Stuart Brotman brings a constructive new perspective to the digital privacy dialogue. Drawing on his extensive background as policy adviser, legal analyst, and business consultant, Stuart brings his unique brand of visionary thinking to bear, synthesizing a fresh multi-stakeholder approach to digital privacy policy. His insights on how the COVID-19 pandemic will continue to affect digital privacy in the post-pandemic world are especially prescient. Stuart moves far beyond conventional wisdom in this fascinating and thought-provoking collection of essays. A "must read" for anyone who cares about digital privacy in all its facets—and wants to be ready for what lies ahead.

Richard T. Kaplar
President and CEO
The Media Institute

The next big thing in technology won't be another Internet-enabled device or service. It will be the long-delayed regulation of Internet society and its new challenges. Chief among these challenges is the privacy problem. Stuart Brotman's collection of essays is both an essential guide to understanding the digital privacy policy landscape and a persuasive argument that the way forward demands a flexible multi-stakeholder approach, rather than a "silver bullet" law. A must-read for anyone who cares about how to solve the privacy puzzle—and who wants to be part of the solution.

Margery Kraus
Founder and Executive Chairman
APCO Worldwide

Stuart Brotman provides a futuristic road map to data/privacy solutions. A thought-provoking read.

Andrew Cohen
author, *Challenge Your Assumptions, Change Your World*

Brotman offers an incisive perspective on data privacy. He provides a consistently thoughtful approach to tech regulation, always considering what policies might best serve the public and our digital society. This is a timely and important book.

Professor Margaret Hu
Penn State Law and School of International Affairs

Privacy's Perfect Storm: Digital Policy for Post-Pandemic Times is must reading for three important reasons: first, Stuart Brotman's research and analysis keep us up-to-date on the complexities of the political and social privacy debate; second, his thoughtful recommendations are actionable and should move policy makers worldwide to move collaboratively, transparently, and urgently; and perhaps most importantly, Brotman poses the difficult questions we all should be asking to clarify who is in charge, who will enforce digital privacy policy, and how will we ever feel truly safe in our post-COVID-19 digital world.

Sandra Baer
President and CEO
Personal Cities

Stuart Brotman's book is a must-read for all those of us seeking the next growth horizon in the digital economy—privacy-assured data services and markets—that lie just beyond what the author appropriately calls "privacy's perfect storm." To that end, policy-makers, executives in the for-profit and NGO worlds, and privacy activists should aggressively drive forward the multi-stakeholder approach Brotman recommends. Brotman is charting the right path into the data-driven future. If we want to thrive, we must heed the practical, specific, and undogmatic advice of this seasoned, internationally renowned scholar/professional who demonstrates once again his mastery of diagnosing digital issues in depth, reflecting thoughtful legal, policy, and commercial perspectives alike.

Olaf Groth PhD
Co-author, *Solomon's Code: Humanity
in a World of Thinking Machines*;
CEO, Cambrian Futures, Inc.
Professor of Practice
Hult International Business School and
UC Berkeley Haas School of Business

Stuart Brotman's effort to provide a guide for navigating "Privacy's Perfect Storm" succeeds magnificently. He takes a necessary, but too rare, holistic approach to digital privacy policy, akin to the holistic approach we attempted with the 2010 National Broadband Plan. Rather than accept conventional wisdom at face value, the book instead maps the complexity and nuance that the intersection of technology, economics, and competing international policies naturally entails. The recommendations also wisely extend beyond today's moment, with Brotman's background in government service enabling him to illuminate for readers the importance of political and public consensus to achieve meaningful outcomes over time.

Blair Levin
Executive Director
2010 United States National Broadband Plan

Stuart Brotman's latest work provides lively, topical, and well-informed case studies that will be illuminating for U.S. policy researchers and advocates. His focus on recent precedents and conditions for promoting privacy, security, and competition in markets for basic and advanced services should be welcomed by all those concerned with shaping our digital future.

Professor Patrick Burkart
Texas A&M University
Co-author, *Why Hackers Win:
Power and Disruption in the Network Society*

Stuart Brotman thoroughly tackles a preeminent challenge of the 21ᵗ century—the explosion of data that promises more efficiency and personalized services while threatening our privacy. This book is a must-read not only for policymakers, but for all consumers concerned about their own privacy and what steps are needed to protect it. Communications networks have long posed privacy issues. Yet the laws were designed for an earlier era, and not for the information tsunami that has made user data the currency generating trillions in market value. This book prepares citizens and government alike to address our nation's new reality.

Jonathan S. Adelstein
President and CEO
Wireless Infrastructure Association

Privacy's Perfect Storm

Digital Policy for Post-Pandemic Times

by Stuart N. Brotman

Stuart N. Brotman

Library of Congress Cataloging-in-Publication Data

Brotman, Stuart N., Privacy's Perfect Storm: Digital Policy for Post-Pandemic Times, privacy, cybersecurity, COVID-19

Summary: The COVID-19 pandemic has expanded the online world of work at home to record levels. Our most personal and confidential data is being collected from multiple digital devices and stored, disseminated, and sold to governments and commercial organizations, often without our knowledge, consent, or control. We are all now in privacy's perfect storm, which includes recent efforts by the European Union and in the United States to set new legal boundaries. Stuart N. Brotman offers a thoughtful guide to achieving better digital privacy protection in these turbulent times.

ISBN: 978-1-939282-48-4

Published by Miniver Press, LLC, McLean Virginia
Copyright 2020 Stuart N. Brotman

First edition August 2020

Table of Contents

Foreword
by Newton N. Minow

After the terrorist attacks on 9/11, I got a call from then-Secretary of Defense Donald Rumsfeld. I had known him for years and he had served as our Congressman. He asked me to chair a new Technology and Privacy Advisory Committee (TAPAC) to help the DoD with one of its most difficult issues. How could the government get the information it needed to protect our citizens from attacks while preserving the privacy rights those citizens rightly considered the very essence of liberty? How much freedom would we have to give up to preserve whatever freedom was left?

TAPAC was chartered in March 2003 "to report on the use of advanced information technologies to help identify terrorists before they act and to identify safeguards to ensure that such technologies comply with U.S. law and American values related to privacy." Our bipartisan group included lawyers and scholars: Floyd Abrams, Zoë Baird, Griffin Bell, Gerhard Casper, William T. Coleman, Jr., Lloyd N. Cutler, and John O. Marsh, Jr. We presented our findings and recommendations in March 2004. The report was titled *Safeguarding Privacy in the Fight Against Terrorism*. We supported the goals of DoD's Terrorism Information Awareness (TIA) program but raised concerns about its implementation, noting that "the same technologies that make data mining feasible can be used to reduce the amount of personally identifiable data necessary."

Furthermore, the law never keeps up with technological developments. From our 2004 report: "Existing legal requirements applicable to the government's many data mining programs are numerous, but disjointed and often outdated, and as a result may compromise the protection of privacy, public confidence, and the nation's ability to craft effective and lawful responses to terrorism."

Very little progress has been made as a matter of policy or legislation since then, as technology has vastly expanded intrusions into our privacy by government and by private entities like corporations. Excellent documentaries like "The Great Hack" and "Zero Days" show us the vulnerability of our data networks. "The Great Hack" begins with a man buying a cup of coffee in a bodega. As he leaves, we see all of the data about the transaction—where he is, what he bought, how he paid for it—being vacuumed up. Corporations and political campaigns will now be able to send him targeted ads. And the government will be able to track his movements. Now imagine that kind of information with every transaction he makes sent to dozens of unseen entities who will see his contributions to nonprofits, whether he is paleo or gluten-free, the countries he calls or visits, the medications he takes, the Facebook posts he likes, and the ones that make him click on the angry symbol.

This is not a new problem. The TAPAC report quoted Alexander Hamilton, who wrote in *Federalist Paper 8* in 1787 that "[s]afety from external danger is the most powerful director of national conduct. Even the ardent love of liberty will, after a time, give way to its dictates ... To be more safe," he concluded, nations "at length become willing to run the risk of being less free." And we cited the U.S. Supreme Court, which wrote in 1963 that it is "under the pressing exigencies of crisis, that there is the greatest temptation to dispense with fundamental constitutional guarantees which, it is feared, will inhibit governmental action."

As Stuart N. Brotman's timely and thoughtful book shows, COVID-19 has had the same effect as the 9/11 terrorism attack in reraising the questions we failed to resolve last time, again in an atmosphere of urgency—this time medical, political, and economic. Like terrorism, a virus cannot be vanquished by traditional means. You can't just declare war and arm the military. With this virus, even our friends and family can suddenly seem like the enemy. Advice columns are filled with letters from people who are anxious because their friends and families do not uphold their standards of handwashing and social distancing.

There is no one way to value privacy and no one way to estimate the risks of failing to get the epidemiological information that could reduce the infection and mortality rate from COVID-19. Someday a vaccine will be found and we can look at the ways other countries have handled it and do better next time. Until that happens, guidance like Brotman's call for a clearer understanding of who has access to what information about us provides a critical template for making sure that we protect our citizens' essential freedoms as well as their safety.

Newton N. Minow is Senior Counsel at Sidley Austin LLP. He served as Chairman of the Federal Communications Commission, PBS, the Carnegie Corporation of New York, and the RAND Corporation.

Stuart N. Brotman

Introduction

IBM estimates we are generating quintillions of digital bytes of data every day—a number followed by thirty zeros. According to Cameron Kerry at The Brookings Institution Center for Technology Innovation, "[t]his explosion is generated by the doubling of computer processing power every 18–24 months that has driven growth in information technology throughout the computer age, now compounded by the billions of devices that collect and transmit data, storage devices and data centers that make it cheaper and easier to keep the data from these devices, greater bandwidth to move that data faster, and more powerful and sophisticated software to extract information from this mass of data. All this is both enabled and magnified by the singularity of network effects—the value that is added by being connected to others in a network—in ways we are still learning."

Current U.S. privacy laws were designed to address the collection and storage of structured data by government, businesses, and other organizations, rather than this ever-expanding data tsunami. They were developed as a series of responses to specific concerns, a checkerboard of federal and state laws, common law jurisprudence, and public and private enforcement that has built up over more than a century.

U.S. privacy laws also are too narrow in protecting "personally identifiable information." The aggregation and correlation of data from various sources make it increasingly possible to link supposedly anonymous information to specific individuals and to infer characteristics and information about them. The result is that a widening range of data has the potential to be personal information (i.e., to identify us uniquely). Few laws or regulations address this new reality, however.

Today, almost every aspect of our lives is in the hands of some third party somewhere. This challenges judgments about reasonable "expectations of privacy" that have been a major premise for defining the scope of U.S. privacy protection for over 100 years. But these judgments present binary choices under this analytic framework: if private information is somehow public or in the hands of a third party, people often are deemed to have no expectation of privacy. This is particularly true when it comes to government access to information—emails, for example, are nominally less protected under our laws once they have been stored 180 days or more, and articles and activities in plain sight are considered categorically available to government authorities. But the concept also gets applied to commercial data in terms and conditions of service and to the scraping of information on public websites.

So as the data universe keeps expanding, more and more of it falls outside the various specific laws on the books. This includes most of the data we generate through such widespread uses as web searches, social media, e-commerce, and smartphone apps. The changes are coming faster than legislation or regulatory rules can adapt, and they erase the sectoral boundaries (e.g., financial, medical) that have largely defined our current privacy laws. It makes little sense that protection of data should depend entirely on who happens to hold it. This arbitrariness will spread as more and more connected devices are embedded in everything from clothing to cars to home appliances to street furniture—the Internet of things.

The U.S. Supreme Court, in its 2018 *Carpenter v. United States* decision, recognized how constant streams of data about us change the ways that privacy should be protected. In holding that law enforcement acquisition of cell phone location records requires a warrant, the Court considered the "detailed, encyclopedic, and effortlessly compiled" information available from cell service location records and "the seismic shifts in digital technology" that made these records available. It concluded that people do not necessarily surrender privacy interests to collect data they generate or by engaging in behavior that can be observed publicly.

How this landmark privacy decision affects a wide variety of digital evidence will play out in criminal cases rather than in the commercial sector. But viewed in a larger context, this case points to a need for a broader set of norms to protect digital privacy in settings that can make information public.

The independent Pew Research Center has tracked online trust and attitudes toward the Internet and companies online. When Pew probed with surveys and focus groups in 2016, it found that "while many Americans are willing to share personal information in exchange for tangible benefits, they are often cautious about disclosing their information and frequently unhappy about what happens to that information once companies have collected it." Many people are "uncertain, resigned, and annoyed."

The massive Equifax data breach in 2018 highlights this sense of anxiety. It compromised personal identity information of almost 146 million Americans, rippling through the financial system by affecting consumers who never did business with Equifax directly, but who were collaterally damaged by the impact of the company's credit scores on economic life.

The Cambridge Analytica stories that same year unleashed even more intense public attention, including live network TV coverage of Facebook CEO Mark Zuckerberg's congressional testimony. Facebook estimates that Cambridge Analytica was able to leverage its "academic" research into uncovering personal data of some 87 million Americans. With over 2 billion Facebook users worldwide, many more people now have a stake in this issue; tellingly, Mark Zuckerberg's legislative testimony has reverberated outside the U.S., including a testimonial appearance before the European Parliament.

After almost twenty years of the world following the U.S. lead in minimizing Internet privacy rights for consumers in order to facilitate Internet platforms' maximal scaling and scoping of their products and services globally (e.g., Google, Facebook), the privacy pendulum has begun to reverse direction.

In May 2018, the EU commenced implementation of its General Data Protection Regulation (GDPR), which covers the EU's 512 million citizens and 411 million Internet users, The EU concluded that what was best for EU consumers and businesses, and for foreign firms doing business in the EU, would be a single comprehensive and consistent EU GDPR standard, instead of a privacy approach with twenty-eight EU countries' partial and inconsistent rules protecting different nations. The EU opted in favor of a more comprehensive, clear, consistent, and efficient privacy protection approach.

The European Union's (EU) General Data Protection Regulation (GDPR) turned one year old in May 2019. U.S. companies are directly in the crosshairs. Whether based in the EU or not, a company is potentially subject to the GDPR (and its stiff fines up to four percent of annual global revenue) if it offers goods or services to data subjects located in the EU, or monitors individuals' online behavior or personal information in the EU. This means that a U.S. company engaged in the common business practice of collecting digital data from its EU customers must assess and implement business practices to ensure GDPR compliance.

There is a growing list of U.S. companies already subjected to GDPR-related EU regulatory actions, including, Amazon, Apple, Facebook, Google, Netflix, Spotify and Twitter. The risks that U.S. companies must manage include measures taken to protect, process, and transfer personal data from the EU to the U.S. in connection with regulatory investigations or litigation.

The most prominent U.S. law in place is the California Consumer Privacy Act (CCPA), which became effective on January 1, 2020. It creates rights for California's 40 million residents to access, correct, delete, and opt out of the sale of personal information. It applies to all businesses that operate in California but exempts those that do not meet minimum revenue or size requirements. The implementing regulations for this law will be issued July 2020, and a more stringent version may be a ballot initiative in the 2020 elections in November.

For many U.S. businesses, the costs of CCPA compliance could exceed that of the GDPR.

How Europe and California regulate data privacy has enormous implications for the United States. EU countries are collectively the largest U.S. trading partner (over $1.3 trillion dollars in trade annually, and California, the most populous state in the U.S., makes up approximately 14% of U.S. GDP.

The CCPA has another and potentially more complicated effect—not only does it induce compliance costs in California, but it also has influenced other states to consider similar or competing privacy legislation, with Maine and Nevada now having their own laws in place. And the next five most populated states—New York, Texas, Florida, Illinois, Pennsylvania have assembled privacy taskforces, introduced bills, or initiated legislative committee reviews which are already under way. There is a growing list of U.S. companies already subjected to GDPR-related EU regulatory actions, including, Amazon, Apple, Facebook, Google, Netflix, Spotify, and Twitter. The risks to U.S. companies include measures taken to protect, process, and transfer personal data from the EU to the U.S. in connection with regulatory investigations or litigation.

The GDPR and CCPA have helped shape both the interest in, and the scope of, potential privacy legislation. So too has the COVID-19 pandemic, as much of the U.S. workforce, public and private education, and personal communications have gone online. This has created greater possibilities for hacking and an increased anxiety regarding digital data collection undertaken for contact tracing and other methods of tracking based on personally identifiable information.

These developments have created a palpable pressure on U.S. policymakers to adopt comparable national legislation; so far, only a handful of states (notably, California, which would have the 5ᵗʰ largest economy if it was a country) has been willing to fill the void until a fully federal approach is developed.

The chair of the U.S. Senate Commerce Committee, John Thune (R-SD) said "many of my colleagues on both sides of the aisle have been willing to defer to tech companies' efforts to regulate themselves, but this may be changing." A number of companies have been increasingly open to a discussion of a basic federal privacy law, as well. Most notably, Facebook's Mark Zuckerberg told CNN, "I'm not sure we shouldn't be regulated," and Apple's Tim Cook has expressed his strong belief that self-regulation is no longer a viable option.

For multinational companies that have spent two years gearing up for compliance with the new data protection law that has taken effect in the EU, dealing with a comprehensive U.S. law no longer looks as daunting. More companies are beginning to see value of a common legal framework that can provide people with reassurance about how their digital data is handled and protected against outliers and outlaws.

Nearly thirty years ago, three major meteorological forces combined in a dramatic and unanticipated way. A barometric low-pressure system, a high-pressure system, and the fading Hurricane Grace collided over the Atlantic Ocean to create havoc on the coast of the Northeast, with Gloucester, Massachusetts at its epicenter. The National Weather Service dubbed this "the Perfect Storm" to convey the unusual and powerful nature of the confluence of these forces.

Since then, this phrase has become part of our lexicon. In a colloquial sense, it now applies to any combination of major forces that overlap at a moment in time to create a reality that is far greater than if the individual forces just played out in an individual way.

The GDPR, the CCPA, and the "new normal" that is sure to be part of the aftermath of the global COVID-19 pandemic are the forces that now represent our nation's critical moment in time for digital privacy. They are "Privacy's Perfect Storm."

During my academic year residency in the Science and Technology Innovation Program at the Wilson Center in Washington, DC, I had a unique vantage point to observe how these forces were affecting a range of stakeholders, including government policymakers, the private sector, NGOs and, of course, the public at large. Various points of view are conveyed by them respectively every day in the nation's capital, all with an eye toward advocacy of particular positions and preferred legislative outcomes.

There is uncertainty about when any U.S. federal legislation will pass, and how much control Internet platforms will concede to consumers to prevent the avoidable alternative of U.S. state data protection legislation for both consumers and businesses, which now is being considered in some way by over twenty states. Any U.S. privacy legislation in the foreseeable future, however, could be designed to preempt or effectively supersede state Internet-related privacy laws, creating tensions in the federal-state allocation of power under the U.S. Constitution.

Government policymakers in Washington, DC increasingly may find themselves between the proverbial rock and a hard place. Similar to another current policy paradox on Capitol Hill—the movement to reduce government spending but wanting to do so without cutting large entitlement programs—it presents a difficult policy and political challenge. How should the right balance be achieved between a seemingly insatiable demand for more widespread online access and a growing anxiety that this access is a primary cause for the erosion of personal privacy?

As the Wilson Center's first-ever Fellow to focus on digital privacy policy, I was able to listen to all these voices with interest and respect, and also review pertinent data and research to inform my thinking. I realized that there needed to be a perspective that was broader in its reach, and in many respects, not tied into a particular legislative bill that was being developed or introduced. On a weekly basis throughout my fellowship, I researched and wrote a new essay to sometimes challenge conventional wisdom, but always to add to the growing conversation about digital privacy protection in a constructive and creative way.

This book organizes the ideas and recommendations articulated in these essays, reflecting challenges and lessons from the COVID-19 pandemic. If anything, the complexities and nuances that I perceived before are now intensified. In light of this, all stakeholders must not just identify problems and positions, but also need to become be part of developing workable the solutions to such a dynamic policy area.

In short, this book is a guide for navigating "Privacy's Perfect Storm." It is written with a sense of optimism and resolve to bring greater meaning to basic principles rooted in longstanding and globally accepted "fair information practices": 1) individual control, 2) transparency, 3) respect for the context in which the data was obtained, 4) access and accuracy, 5) focused collection, 6) security, and 7) accountability.

The COVID-9 pandemic has taught us that with a complex area such as coronavirus contagion, there is unlikely to be a proverbial "silver bullet" that can cover all aspects of it. Rather, social distancing, vigorous hand washing, temperature checks, diagnostic testing, and contact tracing now are recognized as key measures that can help halt its spread. The promised silver bullet of an effective vaccine on a global basis remains an ultimate goal, but there is no current assurance that one can be developed, and even if so, when it would become available.

The holistic public health approach to the pandemic has helped save lives. It also is a concept that is worth emulating in the area of digital privacy policy. Such an approach would differ from the pre-pandemic discussions about "comprehensive" privacy legislation greater detail that has been the focus on Capitol Hill during the past year. This notion assumes that the best route would be to enact a new law that covers a range of digital privacy situation for years to come.

The United States has a significant track record in pursuing a holistic approach to other public policy concerns that is worth reviewing in greater detail. For example, the Centers for Disease Control and Prevention (CDC) has recognized that the reduction of drunk driving nationally will require "different strategies ... [with] different resources for implantation" that may have "different levels of impact." Drunk driving laws are a necessary part of this picture. They have established a nationwide blood alcohol level, and all states and the District of Columbia have raised the minimum drinking age to 21 years old. Local governments also have authorized sobriety checkpoints so police can stop vehicles at highly visible locations to determine if a driver is impaired, followed up by an alcohol breath test if there is a suspicion of intoxication.

But legal measures cannot by themselves provide a sufficient solution. Other stakeholders have joined this effort in positive ways. Various manufacturers have designed and installed ignition interlocks for measuring alcohol levels of repeat DUI offenders, which have proven to be highly effective at preventing new violations from occurring.

Simultaneously, the CDC has advanced multicomponent interventions that combine several programs and/or policies to prevent drunk driving. These include mass media public service campaigns regarding the physical dangers and legal consequences of drunk driving. Persuading people not to drink and drive, or to let others do so, has been an important intervention that complements the new laws aimed at deterrence.

Effective community mobilization through groups such as Mothers Against Drunk Driving (MADD) has also been part of a comprehensive approach to this problem So too are school-based instructional programs that teach teens not to ride with drunk drivers, and the identification by health care, university personnel, and others of people who are at risk for alcohol problems, along with assistance for treatment if needed. The marketplace also has responded through extensive on demand ride services such as Uber and Lyft that are available to transport people who are too intoxicated to drive home safely.

This multidimensional approach can be found in a number of other areas, including the reduction in tobacco use, the increased utilization of seat belts, and preventing wildfires. It suggests that digital privacy policy also could be developed strategically with multiple reinforcing pathways. Legal protections alone, while comprehensive in concept, are unlikely to represent a comprehensive solution in practice. Like drunk driving or these other areas, there are inherent limitations to the reach of legal or regulatory penalties, which need to be assessed more carefully.

The experience of the European Union (EU) since its General Data Protection Regulation (GDPR) took effect in May 2018 illustrates that legislation and regulation may not be as effective as envisioned, and in any event, more time may be needed to assess their real impact on providing better digital privacy protection.

According to POLITICO, in the two years since the GDPR took effect, almost 300,000 complaints have been filed in the EU's twenty-seven countries. With about $325 million allocated for government enforcement during this period, European privacy regulators have levied about $163 million in fines. The result—"two years since the EU's flagship policy regime came online, Silicon Valley's biggest names remain largely unscathed despite a volley of complaints." According to Estelle Massé, Senior Policy Analyst and Policy Analyst and Global Data Protection Lead at Access Now, a civil rights NGO, "Crippled by a lack of resources, tight budgets, and administrative hurdles, [EU] Data Protection Authorities have not yet been able to enforce the GDPR adequately."

At the least, and especially as enforcement funding may not be as abundant in post-pandemic times, legislation and regulation need to establish appropriate public expectations regarding their efficacy, while also building in sufficient time after enactment to evaluate if further fine-tuning may be necessary. We also must aim to satisfy both sides of the dynamic supply and demand equation for Internet services—now and in the future—to enrich our economies, our communities, and our daily lives.

These observations have led me to focus on the need for a multi-stakeholder digital privacy policy toolkit that will be broader and more durable than any particular legislative or regulatory approach might be. In other words, let's de-emphasize a silver bullet approach.

My ideas about engaging governments, public institutions, the private sector, NGOs, and citizens at large are not intended to be exhaustive. Rather, I offer them to help expand the larger political and social conversations that are necessary to provide greater digital privacy protection over time.

Given the constantly changing technological developments at play, I also recognize that it will be important to develop policy implementation with different phases, in order to keep pace with these technologies. Equally important, it might be wise to defer imposing the same laws and regulations on digital technologies that still are in their infancy, which will not deter the beneficial innovation that often occurs in the early stages of marketplace development.

Legislation and regulation at any level clearly will require vigorous oversight and updating, rather than staying in place for decades without necessary modification. Here, the success of "sunset" provisions in various laws is useful to consider, which would require periodic (e.g., every 3–5 years) reauthorization after an evaluation of past practices and future trends has been undertaken.

There can be no doubt now that digital privacy protection deserves more focus as a national policy priority. The essays that follow reflect what I hope will be a common aspiration for all of us. Our nation needs to chart a way forward in a brave new, post-pandemic world that will increasingly be experienced online, both at work and at home.

Thinking About Digital Privacy Protection
in Pandemic Times

The new normal of COVID-19 is for all of us to stay connected on as close to a 24/7 basis as possible. That means having a mobile phone handy wherever we are and wherever we go. The public health demands of tracking such critical aspects as social distancing and virus spreading through contacts has placed a greater potential need for data to be collected and shared by private Internet and telecommunications companies. Such data can be invaluable to government agencies involved in public health planning and implementation during the pandemic.

Other democratic countries such as Israel already have government orders in place that require companies that provide location tracking to turn data over for public health analysis. So far, the United States has not pursued this course. Rather, it still remains in active discussions regarding why and how such data should be made available to relevant government agencies.

Even absent a government mandate, it is hard to imagine that major companies collecting this data will not fully cooperate if and when specific requests are made, with the strong justification that such information may help stem the dramatic increase of diagnosed cases and the increased number of deaths that are sure to follow.

That's why now is the time for government and the private sector to develop clear transparency rules when these data transfers take place. Transparency in general is one of the cornerstones in gaining public confidence during this crisis. Such confidence may erode if individuals feel that our nation is becoming a surveillance state.

Location tracking data, while collected individually, will only have value here if it is compiled in the aggregate, so that trends can be mapped in determining public health recommendations and outcomes. This already has been useful in collecting cell tower pings in Kenya to predict the spread of malaria. In the U.S., there are even more precise ways to track locations based on apps and telecommunications operating systems.

But users need to be assured that these practices do not fall into the category of personally identifiable information that current and future privacy laws are intended to protect. Typical users are not aware of this distinction. This places the burden on the government and the private sector to provide details about the collection and dissemination of anonymous, aggregated data. Word about this must be communicated clearly and quickly.

As a practical matter, transparency also should include a requirement that companies providing location tracking data modify their user agreements, as needed, to reflect this practice. Additionally, these companies and all involved government agencies—whether federal, state, or local—should be required to visibly post their disclosures on websites, apps, and social media.

Digital transparency is important in the coming days, but it may need additional measures to dissuade bad actors from reverse engineering these aggregated data to discover individual identities for exploitation directly or through third parties. This may call for accompanying tighter controls for transferring the data between companies and government agencies, and possible criminal or civil penalties for those involved in malicious reverse engineering.

The emergency circumstances at play now require marshaling all resources to help fight the pandemic. Yet even here, informing the public about the limited use of collected digital data for aggregated analysis will reflect both good policy and good sense.

Stuart N. Brotman

Why Discussing Digital Privacy
Now Belongs at the Kitchen Table

As we huddle in our homes for remote work, schooling, and family life, our nation has been dramatically transformed within weeks to one that operates largely online, as millions are tethered to their screens on various digital devices for most waking hours.

This increasing use of, and dependence on, broadband networks, websites, and apps enable us to undertake daily activities while social distancing from others who are not hunkered down with us. Whether we are applying for a new job, seeking government financial assistance, or enabling telehealth diagnoses, there is no doubt that digital privacy finally has reached the kitchen table.

The kitchen table metaphor is a staple of politics—people care most about issues that affect their livelihoods, health care, and education. This makes sense because it reflects a set of public policy concerns that are of the highest priority to the broadest range of citizens. Government officials at all levels, especially those who serve at the pleasure of voters, understandably are sensitive to kitchen table issues because they are a proxy for what matters most to vast numbers of people.

Anyone who ever has attended or viewed a town hall with candidates of either party has seen kitchen table issues prominently on display. Will jobs continue to decline? Will health care be accessible and affordable? What will be the burdens of student debt? These topics invariably have dominated such sessions, as they should. But going forward, they will be filtered through the lens of a post-pandemic United States, where all of these concerns will be both more acute and more difficult to address given the uncertainties that COVID-19 has brought with it.

Digital privacy has been much discussed in Europe: when the European Union enacted the General Data Protection Regulation (GDPR) in 2018; in California, when the California Consumer Privacy Act (CCPA) took effect at the beginning of this year; in over twenty additional states considering legislation; and in Congress. There are various legal and policy proposals that have been raised but not finalized so far. The challenges of national COVID-19 recovery, however, may put some of these on the back burner for the rest of 2020, and perhaps beyond.

Ironically, this retreat might come at a time when more citizens of all ages throughout the country are becoming more sensitive to digital privacy concerns. The intensity of our online lives, the variety of digital devices, and the large increase in the collection, storage, and dissemination of personally identifiable information is bringing digital privacy to the kitchen table as never before. Even increasing public health measures such as virus contact tracing through location tracking underscore that virtually all aspects of working, studying, and staying healthy now involve risks to the security of our informational identities. And not surprisingly, bad actors are ready to take advantage of the national emergency through phishing, malware, and more aggressive hacking activities.

But in crisis, there is also opportunity. Sheltered in place, Americans now are uniquely positioned to have kitchen table conversations—yes, at the kitchen table itself—with all members of their household. How is each person interacting online, and what measures should they be taking to help protect their own transmission of sensitive information? What informational requests are they receiving from others? How vital will this information be to getting or keeping a job, completing coursework, or receiving timely heath care?

Equally important, once these candid conversations take place among family members, will be to share digital privacy perspectives with elected representatives and their challengers throughout the 2020 election year. This includes asking questions about digital privacy in town hall sessions, including those that will take place virtually instead of in crowded community centers.

Policy approaches for digital privacy protection so far have largely been formulated from the top down, with little input from the public at large regarding their actual concerns about greater digital privacy protection. With this issue now among those meriting serious discussion at the kitchen table, the stage has been set to formulate digital privacy boundaries that reflect important real-world concerns and practices.

In turn, this input and feedback can help ensure that digital privacy protection remains top of mind for government officials as a critical aspect of COVID-19 recovery. Our new base of collective experience can help sharpen the focus of policy makers addressing this issue, by enabling a more complete perspective regarding what greater privacy protections will be needed in our permanently expanded digital lives.

Stuart N. Brotman

Let's Utilize Our Best Digital Messengers for Pandemic Public Health Information

With the United States, like the rest of the world, consumed with the rapid spread of COVID-19, necessary attention to public health assessments and forecasts is critical. Public health responses are essential to flatten the growth curve for the virus, enable widespread testing, and allocate resources for sufficient medical professionals and hospitals. Now is the time for the federal government to assess its role as a public health messenger, since digital trust will be a necessary aspect of dealing with this crisis, too.

We need to understand that the public health information that is being received is being filtered by a pervasive level of distrust of news and information in general, and specifically trust in government. Increasingly, this news and information is being transmitted online, including through various social media platforms.

According to a Pew Research Center survey conducted in the past year, nearly seven-in-ten U.S. adults say made-up news and information greatly impacts Americans' confidence in government institutions. This is a dismal sign indeed. The COVID-19 pandemic is taking place against a broad reality that the public health information being received—however evidence-based—must first penetrate a layer of public skepticism and cynicism about the messenger itself. This is counterproductive to swift and decisive recommendations that may not be followed as a result.

Other data, however, suggest possibilities for utilizing alternative ways to alert the public online about the virus generally and preventive measures specifically. Here, the 20ᵗʰ annual Edelman Trust Barometer, a survey index released just a few weeks ago, can serve as a quick reference source for exploring other options.

It reflects another bit of bad news. The Barometer indicates that there are two groups that need to be addressed. The first is what is called the "informed public," which comprises less than 20% of the mass population. But their socioeconomic metrics— those ages 25–64, college educated, and in the top 25% of household incomes—clearly separate them from the rest of the country. And the mass population also does not reflect significant media consumption or engagement in public policy and business news. That's why it is so important that vital public health information reaches both groups impactfully.

Despite the trust gap between them, half of all Americans trust nongovernment organizations (NGOs) and businesses, while only about 40% trust government. And within government, local and state government is trusted more than the federal government.

Two quick recommendations flow from viewing the Pew Research Center and Edelman surveys in tandem. First, it would be helpful to have COVID-19 public health information immediately amplified by NGOs and businesses through their websites and social media. This can help reinforce the credibility of that information. Second, the preferable government pathway for this information should be local and state officials, including, governors, mayors, and school superintendents.

Creating greater digital information trust is a larger and broader social problem that needs to be addressed in the long term, of course. For now, having the right online messengers front and center clearly can be part of a comprehensive approach to the pandemic that is our new normal.

Limiting Personal Information
in Our Post-Pandemic "New Normal"

With so much uncertainty regarding when the COVID-19 pandemic will subside sufficiently to allow people to return to work, including retail work, there seems to be a clear consensus that what lies ahead on the other side is an unknown world known as the "new normal."

Although the contours of future business and social interactions remain undefined, they seem likely to require more hand washing throughout the day, distancing in office spaces and restaurants, and probably the permanent disappearance of the hearty handshake for greetings and departures.

Given the vast increase in the use of, and dependency upon, digital connections at home now, along with an increased need for government surveillance to facilitate contact tracing through location tracking, there also will be an understandable growing sensitivity to how much personally identifiable information is being collected, stored, and disseminated—especially after the virus subsides or can be dealt with through effective treatments or a vaccine.

So here's quick recommendation that Congress could adopt in any of its upcoming COVID-19 funding packages: prohibit the use by any nonfederal governmental entity from using a Social Security number as a personal identifier. The unrestricted requests for these numbers seemingly are made any time we fill out a form online. But why?

This identification system was created by law in 1936 for the sole purpose of tracking the earnings histories of U.S. workers to determine their entitlement to Social Security benefits and compute their benefit levels. Today, the Social Security Administration (SSA) has issued over 450 million assigned numbers to nearly every legal resident in the United States. According to the SSA, this "very universality has led to its adoption throughout government and the private sector as a chief means of identifying and gathering information about an individual."

As we begin to plan for a new normal, it's time to return to the original intent of Social Security numbers, by limiting their widespread use for unintended and unauthorized purposes as an unofficial national identifier.

The SSA itself acknowledges that every year, "millions of Americans become victims of identity theft. Identity theft occurs when someone steals your personally identifiable information and pretends to be you. They can use this information to open bank or credit card accounts, file taxes, or make new purchases in your name." In our post-pandemic world, it's likely that bad actors will ramp up their identity theft activities, and Social Security numbers can be keys that unlock doors that have a wealth of personal information behind them.

This means that restricting the use of these numbers to the Social Security system itself can help stem the flow of dire economic consequences—both for individuals and businesses—when these numbers are acquired through hacking, malware, and the like. And there is no countervailing public policy reason why the current widespread use of these numbers should continue, especially since the law is clear about the limits that Congress intended when it acted over eighty years ago.

The Privacy Act of 1974, which gave citizens protection from certain information disclosures and a right to review and fix their own records, also created an enduring gap by not including Social Security number requests made by businesses and nonfederal agencies. In effect, this shifted the burden to individuals to refuse giving over their number when asked for it by these entities. But as a practical matter, how many of us have ever exercised this right of refusal, especially since it could lead to a withholding of benefits by a requesting provider?

Congress recognized this problem, in part, when it enacted a subsequent law thirty years later that bars states from putting Social Security numbers on drivers' licenses, identification cards, or vehicle registrations. These prohibitions have been on place since 2005, and have clearly demonstrated that massive processing of individual information is possible without using these numbers.

In the new normal, the logical next step should move beyond these laws to explicitly discontinue the use of Social Security numbers for many unintended purposes. Let's have Congress establish a permanent prohibition, along with penalties that provide real teeth for the widespread use of Social Security numbers.

States already have shown that they can develop their own alternate identification systems for more tailored purposes. The American private sector, rooted deeply in innovation and competition, also can develop comparable individual identifiers that do not rely on Social Security numbers. The upside of this change would be welcomed by the public at large as we navigates through a brave new world where better privacy protection can become an unintended positive outcome from the unprecedented public health crisis that we are all enduring.

Deploying U.S. Artificial Intelligence Leadership for COVID-19—Competitively and Cooperatively

Among the cutting-edge technologies being employed by public health experts to map various aspects of COVID-19, both at home and abroad, artificial intelligence (AI) faces a test under life-and-death circumstances. The ability of AI systems to undertake pattern detection and make predictions concerning the spread of the pandemic and its treatments is promising, but also limited by the nature of machine learning—analysis of historical data to find key variables. This task is dependent upon humans, however, specifically the ability of data scientists who can work on creating data sets that supercomputers then can model. On a global basis, this will require pooling both technical and human resources.

Given the unprecedented nature of COVID-19, historic data inputted for AI analysis may be of limited value. Real-time data comparing growth curves in countries around the world, along with population and demographic information by neighborhood, may prove to be a better vein for producing actionable data anywhere and everywhere. Automated machine learning also may improve the efficiency of data scientists, enabling them to focus on new data generation while relying on computer-to-computer analysis of massive-scale number crunching.

According to the Center for Data Innovation, as of last summer, the United States and China are emerging as the two country competitors for global AI leadership. China's aspirations are explicit: it seeks to achieve AI dominance both to expand its economic footprint and to fortify its military power.

The Center's analysis indicates that so far, the U.S. is leading this race, including in areas such as talent, research and development, and hardware. One critical aspect for our nation is in the area of innovation, which is the beneficiary of a robust private equity and venture funding capability. Another is our significant strength both in traditional semiconductors and AI-specific computer chips. China is leading in AI system adoption and in AI data production, which also are important assets.

COVID-19 presents an opportunity to demonstrate in practice what various comparative metrics aim to convey. It also will reveal longer-term issues regarding how the U.S. may fall behind in AI development if it does not bulk up in its stronger advantages and shore up some of its weaker competitive areas during this crisis. Federal stimulus funding to help address pandemic concerns could increase incentives for AI research and development, for example. This could take the form of direct subsidies for focused R&D, tax credits, or some combination of these.

Money alone will not be sufficient. We also must be mindful that more and better domestic AI talent must be developed at America's great research universities, with more academic research funding clearly necessary to enhance an enlarged homegrown AI talent pipeline.

The Center's report is correct in noting that "the race to develop or adopt AI is not a zero sum game ... And many AI advancements, particularly those focused on health ... can benefit all countries. For example, the development of AI systems that can identify diseases faster and more accurately than clinicians, or produce new medical treatments, offers potentially global benefits."

Competition aside, this means that the larger common task we share now with China may be more important now than our ongoing trade disputes, which have resulted in the imposition of tariffs on select goods imported by each country. U.S. and China AI players have an opportunity to pool technical resources and know-how, particularly since the strengths of both countries complement each other. Collectively, they also are in a good position to learn from advancements in the EU, including the work of data scientists in Italy, who have access to unique data based on the rapid spread of COVID-19 there. That's because much AI research is shared openly already. And the possibility of limited, royalty-free cross-licensing of AI patents held by the U.S. and China may be especially beneficial to bring in much-needed technical capability on a short-term basis.

This ability to compete and cooperate simultaneously can achieve win-win outcomes both sooner and later. The United States should send a clear signal to China soon that it is open to explore AI working arrangements that will not just benefit the economies and strategic interests of both countries, but also help achieve the global goal of successfully confronting a worldwide pandemic with the best AI tools that can be brought to bear.

Stuart N. Brotman

Privacy and Cybersecurity Support is Essential for Small Businesses Pandemic Fighting

The U.S. Small Business Administration (SBA) is playing a pivotal role in helping to keep our nation's economy afloat during the COVID-19 pandemic. Its critical concern is financial, of course, which includes assisting small businesses in meeting payrolls and covering rent, insurance, and other essential obligations. Congress already has allocated hundreds of millions of dollars for a Paycheck Protection Program, Economic Injury Disaster Loans, and Loan Advances and Bridge Loans. Hopefully, these will provide some much-needed short-term relief to allow continued operations, albeit on a reduced scale, and provide a buffer against bankruptcy in the coming months. The SBA also has been helpful in identifying common small business issues that will be encountered during this unprecedented public health crisis. These include inventory and supply chain shortfalls, facility remediation, and changing market demand.

Many small businesses, however, are providing services, not goods, and their employees now have been largely moved out of company locations to residential environments, where extensive telework is taking place. This means that it will be largely up to individual businesses to make that transition on their own, without the explicit support of the SBA or the resources that are available to larger corporate entities.

This is particularly the case for information technology (IT). Most small businesses probably do not have full-time IT departments that are responsible for hardware and software selection and bulk purchasing, dealing with malware issues, and overseeing network management (including private intranets as well as the public Internet). Instead, they now must rely primarily on their employees' own computer devices, their residential broadband services of varying quality, and different levels of sophistication regarding how to protect the digital information that they are transmitting and receiving.

It's unclear how small businesses are prepared for this seismic shift. Small company networks, if they exist, may not be adequately protected from system contamination. Viruses of a different kind may be spread to company employees working at home (and vice versa). The private devices these employees are using also may be unprotected, leaving open greater opportunities for foreign and domestic hackers to create all types of digital disruptions, including fake news alerts that induce greater public panic. And the increased social isolation among new mandatory teleworkers will mean that more sensitive personal information beyond the business context will be sent to family and friends. Their decreased sensitivity to digital privacy concerns then can bleed into daily work activities.

The SBA can act now to help with these problems. First, in administering its various loan programs that now have been funded, the agency should include financing and upgrading of IT systems for residential use as a line item for borrowing, along with associated costs for teleworker training to enable a uniform, higher level of employee digital privacy protection measures. Required, time-limited strong passwords and two-factor authentication are examples of these measures, and they should be applied to all online text and video capabilities that employees are using at home. Independent contractors involved in telework also should be required to follow the same protocols as employees.

Raising awareness about these issues can be valuable too, especially as small businesses turn to the SBA as a trusted source for advice as well as money. Here, the SBA should add digital privacy and cybersecurity on its website as one of its highlighted COVID-19 concerns for small businesses.

These approaches are particularly timely as funding guidelines are being drafted. And adding a few lines to a webpage can be accomplished in a matter of minutes. They may not save lives, but they can make a real difference in sustaining small businesses, especially given their increasingly intense reliance on digital technologies and the Internet.

Stuart N. Brotman

Why Congress Needs to Address Technology
in the Next Relief Bill

The steps toward another stimulus package have begun in earnest, with signals from the White House and Congress that infrastructure deserves a higher priority in a new round of spending. This bipartisan support will need other voices to enact legislation to expand and improve our energy grid, water systems, and broadband networks. Few will be able to argue that our leaders are operating optimally to meet future demands, given the critical role infrastructure will play to bring our economy back to life. Such an effort will require a hefty price tag of $1 trillion or more.

One item that must be tucked into relief legislation is the reestablishment of the Office of Technology Assessment. It was extinguished twenty-five years ago, based on the premise that Congress need not have better expertise when evaluating the technological implications of legislation in its pipeline. The Office of Technology Assessment received $22 million annually at its peak funding. Its defunding was done with a bad sense that even this miniscule amount was still too much to spend to ensure that Congress could remain up to speed on technological developments. The coming era, which was characterized by a technological tsunami in the United States and around the world, has now demonstrated the unmindful nature of this decision.

Congress surely would have been more knowledgeable about the technology involved with telework, telehealth, and supply chain operations, all of vital importance in our toolkit to confront the coronavirus, if it had an Office of Technology Assessment today. Hand wringing about the decision to shut it down, however, only looks backward in speculating about previous laws and how to more efficiently spend taxpayer dollars. Congress should now rectify its "penny wise and pound foolish" approach by ensuring that the Office of Technology Assessment is reestablished as soon as possible.

Any funding allocation still would be tiny, not even at the level of budget rounding errors, yet the payoff would be substantial. How will Congress effectively allocate such massive amounts for infrastructure that require detailed information of the technology that comprises its elements? How will Congress provide meaningful oversight for these funds once they are authorized? Beyond infrastructure, of course, is a broader range of other technology with important implications for national security and global trade. Artificial intelligence and blockchain are two key examples here.

Indeed, the Select Committee on the Modernization of Congress last year favorably reviewed whether a renewed Office of Technology Assessment would help provide better expertise to lawmakers. But only $6 million was included in a legislative spending bill to do this, and even this amount was not forthcoming. As the Belfer Center for Science and International Affairs at Harvard University correctly noted, "Congress does not, in fact, lack a supply of folks trying to give it advice. To the contrary, it is overwhelmed. What it lacks is the ability to sort through it all." From this perspective, the Office of Technology Assessment should have a reconstituted mission to recognize the value of new further external information about technology, assimilate it, and assist Congress with applying it to legislative outcomes.

The Office of Technology Assessment can deliver the best bang for the buck if it is able to help our lawmakers with the avalanche of information generated by universities, think tanks, nonprofit groups, and the private sector. Some might argue that other government agencies, such as the Congressional Research Service and Government Accountability Office, can assume this role if provided with some additional funding and staff, therefore minimizing the possibility of including duplicative resources.

But these impressive organizations have such a broad range of topics to cover and are designed to generate new research rather than synthesize the best available technology knowledge for Congress. A lean and mean Office of Technology Assessment, funded for an initial period of five years with a sunset provision to make it palatable, would be a far more attractive option. Whatever the price tag, it holds the promise of being the greatest bargain for our nation that any other relief legislation could now include.

Health Information Technology's National Blueprint for COVID-19

It's been ten years this month since the release of the National Broadband Plan, a 376-page document that was one of the products of the American Recovery and Reinvestment Act of 2009. In our current COVID-19 crisis, its Chapter 10, covering health care, deserves immediate and close attention to determine how its analysis and recommendations might be applicable to the critical decisions that must be made—both in confronting our pandemic and in anticipating the next pandemic to come.

First, let's focus on what the plan revealed that underscores a persistent problem in dealing with COVID-19: "The United States is not taking full advantage of the opportunities that health IT [information technology] provides." Three national gaps were identified that remain today: adoption by health care providers, information utilization by them, and connectivity to patients.

The current crisis certainly must deal with connectivity issues, particularly in rural areas where sparse population density has made construction of high-speed fixed networks to homes economically unattractive and unsustainable for private companies. The reality of a digital divide remains, and it places millions of Americans with inferior access to health information and online educational resources as public schools begin to close en masse. Unfortunately, this structural problem cannot be addressed in real time now. Enabling more mobile broadband connectivity in these unserved or underserved areas, making available more connection hotspots there, and encouraging private sector cooperation in lifting monthly data gaps all can be helpful in the coming weeks and months, however. They can help make more robust broadband connectivity a reality for so many in need.

The more dramatic immediate impact should build upon the plan's analysis, which current circumstances demand. It called for our nation to "marshal support from Congress, states and the health care community to drive e-care use" and to "provide the health IT industry with a clear understanding of the federal government's policies toward e-care."

Here, the reduction of regulatory barriers should be a top priority. Stimulating capital investments may be commercially infeasible, and may take too much time even if large federal grants or loan guarantees are made available. Although some congressional action may be needed, the emphasis should be on executive branch action that can be put in place on an accelerated basis. For example, the Centers for Medicare & Medicaid Services (CMS) of the Department of Health and Human Services, which is the largest financial force in health care delivery, can reduce regulatory barriers that inhibit the adoption of health IT solutions. And the Department's Office of the National Coordinator for Health Information Technology has the power to establish interim common standards and protocols for sharing administrative, research, and clinical data.

As the plan wisely noted, "Video consultation and remote access to patient data may also be critical during pandemic situations. If hospitals are at capacity or if isolation protocols are necessary to prevent the spread of the infection, these technologies can help health care providers assist more patients and help patients avoid public areas."

Adjusting other current high regulatory barriers, at least until the pandemic subsides, is also envisioned in the plan, and would be accepted as common sense today. CMS can revise its standards that make health care credentialing and privileging overly burdensome for e-care. This means that the site where the patient is located is not now allowed to rely on the site where the physician is located for credentialing and privileging the doctor prescribing the care.

States have an important role to play in revising licensing requirements to enable timely e-care, too, so as not to limit practitioners' abilities to treat patients across state lines. The plan suggests that the "nation's governors and state legislatures could collaborate through such groups as the National Governors Association, the National Conference of State Legislatures and the Federation of State Medical Boards." Given the scale and speed of the pandemic, such coordination should be pursued quickly with this focused goal in mind.

A decade ago, the plan asserted, "Health IT enables widespread data capture, which in turn allows better real-time health surveillance and improved response time to update care recommendations, allocate health resources and contain population-wide health threats."

Especially given the bipartisan congressional support it received then, the National Broadband Plan should be a frontline document for government executives and legislators, pulled off the shelf for ideas that can be implemented quickly, then extended in the long term if they prove to be as effective as envisioned.

How Health Information Privacy Lives on During the COVID-19 Pandemic

The COVID-19 pandemic has exposed numerous shortcomings in planning for, and operating during, a global crisis of this magnitude. In the United States, personal protective equipment, ventilators, virus tests, and ICU hospital beds remain in short supply. Public health authorities also have an increased need for more big data so trends can be mapped and resource allocations can be determined on an ongoing basis.

The collection of these data, while justified on national emergency grounds, has also raised concerns regarding how much of it will be collected in aggregate and anonymously, and how much will include sensitive health information to profile individuals who have been infected or have recovered from COVID-19. Contact tracing data may also help determine who has been in direct contact with someone who has tested positive.

The good news is that the U.S. has a well-crafted federal law in place that has served us well for several decades. Although some exceptions are being carved out, given the current emergency, they are being done with precision and respect for the overall bedrock privacy principles for this sensitive category of personal information.

The Health Insurance Portability and Accountability Act (HIPAA), a law enacted during the Clinton administration with broad bipartisan support, is nearly twenty-five years old. It has stood the test of time—even now. The law protects health insurance coverage for workers and their families when they change or lose their jobs, which is vital as unemployment figures skyrocket on a weekly basis.

A central feature of HIPAA that also is critical now, is its Privacy Rule, which regulates the use and disclosure of protected health information (PHI). PHI is any information held by a covered entity regarding health status or health care provisioning that can be linked to any individual (e.g., a medical record or medical payment history). The rule is expansive in defining a covered entity, too; health care clearinghouses, employer-sponsored health plans, health insurers, and medical service providers both within and outside hospitals and clinics are included, as are independent contractors that have business relationships with any of them.

The health care community is required to respect PHI in a number of different, complementary ways. Generally, disclosure by a covered entity requires written authorization from the individual for the disclosure, and in any event, only allows providing the minimum necessary information required to achieve its purpose. A covered entity also must notify individuals regarding how their PHI is being used, and enable an individual to correct any inaccurate PHI.

And there is enforcement of HIPAA through the Department of Health and Human Services Office for Civil Rights, and in some cases, by the Department of Justice Criminal Division. There is some debate regarding how vigorous the enforcement activities have been, given the relatively small amount of human and financial resources at hand to deal with tens of thousands of privacy complaints that are filed each year. This deficiency seems real, and is worthy of a budget increase as part of any COVID-19 funding package that is introduced in the coming weeks.

But even with this situation, HIPAA has had a significant positive impact within the health care community, by creating a respect for personal health information that is greater than other types of personal information. The combination of government policing and covered entity self-policing has created a durable health information ecosystem where relatively few bad faith violations occur, and where public confidence in providing PHI remains high.

COVID-19 presents a real-time stress test to determine how effective HIPAA really is during a crisis of such large magnitude. The need for flexibility in applying the law when emergency circumstances arise was addressed in a 2013 rule change that permits waiver of HIPAA provisions under these circumstances. This was done when Hurricane Harvey struck in 2017, and of course, most recently as COVID-19 rapidly spreads across the country.

Yet even in these circumstances, the HIPAA waiver has not been a blanket one that tips the balance against individuals in favor of government officials who request both general and specific health information to help confront the epidemic. Rather, the general principles of confidentiality and transparency remain intact, while also tailoring a specific enforcement moratorium narrowly. For example, there will not be any penalties for independent contractors that disclose PHI to public health authorities if such disclosure is done in good faith and the health care provider in that relationship is informed within ten business days. But other requirements under the Privacy Rule are still subject to full enforcement, including important security and breach notification requirements.

In short, there seems to be an effective safety net in place regarding the collection and dissemination of PHI. As post-pandemic measures are considered, legislatures would be well advised to consider whether the framework, history, and application of HIPAA's Privacy Rule during these trying times offers a starting point for crafting any new privacy laws that cover personally identifiable information outside the health care realm. We may well have before us a template that can serve as a broader policy foundation once new laws are being developed, whether by individual states or by Congress, if a federal approach is pursued.

Stuart N. Brotman

How Digital Privacy Protection Can Become Compatible With COVID-19 Location Data Tracking

"We are all in this together." This seems to me the mantra as we cope with the COVID-19 pandemic. It's not an aspiration, but rather is an affirmation that individuals and organizations have an unprecedented opportunity to work toward a common goal, in ways that were unimaginable only a few weeks ago.

And the global scale of this public health crisis means that the United States is learning from, and cooperating with, countries around the world. This includes producing and distributing essential medical supplies, working on vaccine development, and sharing large amounts of data to determine virus spread and how best to allocate resources to treat those who become infected.

This general level of cross-sector and international cooperation also should be applied to digital privacy protection. Contact tracing and social distance planning will require that data from digital devices increasingly will be requested by, or volunteered to, public health officials and policymakers at all levels of government. This increased demand for data was not envisioned to become part of a large-scale government surveillance plan, so understandably there is a sense of comfort for some, but unease for others.

Here, the United States should look abroad for possible alternatives to the traditional approach that pits the government against the private sector regarding digital privacy protection. For a view of what such an approach might look like, it is important to observe models from other countries that are trying something different. Exhibit A is Israel. That country imposed mandatory self-quarantine requirements for citizens and noncitizens alike who were arriving at its borders. It also ordered all nonessential businesses to close nearly a month ago, while the U.S. has no such national requirement in place to date.

Notably, Israel also has taken advantage of its technological prowess to gather and disseminate relevant data to government officials, collected individually but used anonymously. Like the United States, Israel is one of the world's leading nations for innovation. Both established and start-up tech companies there are working 24/7 to develop new ways to gather location data beyond such relatively crude methods as cell tower tracking.

Israel has a special lesson to offer the United States regarding how to stimulate workable technology approaches to COVID-19 that also reflect greater sensitivity to digital privacy concerns. A service called Hamgen (The Shield) is a joint effort of private sector tech experts and Israel's Health Ministry. With this cooperative development effort, The Shield devised a solution that would be beneficial to the Health Ministry while also respecting personal privacy protection. The location data from an individual's smartphone is collected from the past fourteen days, then matched with the whereabouts of others in the Health Ministry's database. The result of that process then is made available to the individual, notifying whether he or she has crossed paths with an infected user. If so, the protocol is a voluntary self-quarantine for fourteen days and notification of this to the ministry.

Unlike the U.S., this approach is based on people opting in rather than opting out, providing their location data voluntarily, so that infected individuals are only traced with their knowledge and approval. The personal information and location data remain on personal smartphones rather than stored in a centralized cloud platform.

So far, The Shield has received broad and quick acceptance, with 1.5 million Israelis reportedly downloading the app within the first three days that it became available. About 50,000 users then discovered a territorial match with someone who has COVID-19.

Like social distancing and other measures that require massive public buy-in to achieve a necessary scale that may make a difference, it will take some time to determine how effective The Shield can be. Presumably, it could be made available to the United States and other countries if it yields some positive results in helping to flatten the curve.

In any event, the larger idea seems to be one that could immediately be beneficial. Public health agencies and tech companies of all sizes in the U.S. should follow Israel's lead by working in concert to develop privacy by design approaches. This would help emphasize that it still is possible to continue thinking about digital privacy protection even in these dire times, while enabling the public health community to get better data snapshots regarding how fast and wide COVID-19 is spreading. After all, "We are all in this together."

Stuart N. Brotman

How Persistent is Our Privacy Paradox?

The recently released Pew Research Center report "Americans and Privacy: Concerned, Confused and Feeling Lack of Control Over Their Personal Information" may create an unwanted feeling of uneasiness. It indicates that a "majority of Americans believe their online and offline activities are being tracked and monitored by companies and the government with some regularity." And 60% of surveyed adults "do not think it is possible to go through daily life without having data collected about them by companies or the government."

This study reflects a sense of anxiety about having little or no control over how these entities are using our personal information. Little wonder that in state capitals and on Capitol Hill alike, both Democratic and Republican legislators are searching for government solutions to address this issue. Tech companies, such as Amazon and Facebook, also are echoing a need for new laws that better protect personal information that is collected and disseminated online, then stored in a cloud with endless capacity. But these developments tell only part of the story.

Another seminal study is the EMC Privacy Index, developed in 2014 by the data storage company that now is part of the technology giant Dell. That report found the vast majority of respondents in all surveyed countries, including the United States, indicated that they value the benefit of "easier access to information and knowledge" that digital technology affords. Yet

81% back then also expected privacy to erode over the next five years, which is what the Pew Center research has confirmed in 2019. Today, Pew found that 70% of U.S. adults think that their personal information is less secure than it was five years ago.

The EMC Privacy Index's most impactful finding was that although people worldwide are using digital technology at a high rate, far fewer (only 45%) indicated they were willing to give up *any* of their privacy in exchange for the ability to keep receiving these benefits. This "We Want It All" privacy paradox applies to everyday activities such as searching for nearby stores by enabling geo-location and critical citizen benefits such as protection from terrorists and/or criminals.

How much are we still guided by this behavioral insight a half decade later? Here, the Pew Center research suggests that we may have tipped the balance in the other direction—81% of survey respondents indicated that the potential risks of data collection by companies now outweigh the potential benefits, with 66% noting the risks outweigh the benefits of government data collection. But a majority also appreciates that online ads based on their personal data mirror their interests and characteristics.

On balance, it seems that we still want it all online—extensive technical capabilities and service offerings along with rich privacy protection. That dissonance is one we all must think about individually as we decide what to click on, where and how often, and what to upload, download, or send to others in social media postings.

Although there may be a general sense that control has been lost, increasing attention should be focused on our choices to engage or disconnect, which can help shape the online marketplace. We are also not talking about why we are less concerned, as the Pew Center survey shows, about how government is using our information instead of companies. Why is this so?

It's time to explore how we can pursue behaviors that protect the data we are sharing (better passwords and more frequent changes, anyone?). Legal mechanisms for improving digital privacy protection should remain top of mind for policymakers, but any new laws need to account for how willing the public will be in protecting their own online data when they can.

No statute or government agency will be able to impose this important element collectively.

Digital Trust is Essential
for Data Privacy Protection

As the holiday shopping season builds momentum, Americans await a gift that is much desired but difficult to provide: digital trust. According to the Frost and Sullivan 2018 Global State of Online Digital Trust Survey, 50% of companies have been involved in publicly disclosed data breaches, almost all of which resulted in negative revenue impact and an erosion of consumer trust.

A common perception in the United States is that these data breaches, usually involving sensitive, personally identifiable information, are transitory events to be minimized because they cannot be prevented every time. But this misses an important aspect of the problem—namely, how to build digital trust as companies expand their business models to monetize a dramatically increasing amount of data that is being collected from users.

Here, it is useful to look abroad to see how other countries are building digital trust as a cultural norm and a societal expectation. Although some of these countries have smaller populations, they can be viewed as laboratories for scaling up in the U.S. if a strategic push for greater digital trust among the public at large is to be pursued.

Finland is a case in point. It's ranked third (while the U.S. is ranked eighth) among the most innovative economies in the world by the 2019 Bloomberg Innovation Index. Finland recognizes that digital trust is essential to innovation, and that it entails a series of interconnected elements. For example, Eurostat ranks Finland first in trust in a country's political system, and second in trust in a legal system. Its corporate ethics ranking is comparable too, according to the World Economic Forum.

Finland has not sacrificed business growth by promoting digital trust, either. Again, according to_the World Economic Forum, it ranks second in the world for using information and communication technologies to boost competitiveness *and* well-being. Doing well by doing good is not a contradiction.

Neighboring Estonia was the first country to endure a cyberattack on a national scale. The attack took down banks, media outlets, and government institutions in 2007. Yet since then, it has been named "the most advanced digital society in the world" by WIRED. Estonia now is home to NATO's Cooperative Cyber Defense Centre of Excellence and the European IT Agency. It owns and manages data centers in other countries in order to protect the Estonian Government Cloud. And in a first under international law, these Data Embassies under Estonia's control now have the same diplomatic rights as physical embassies.

Estonians are impressed by these initiatives, and have been supportive of the government's move to provide 99% of public services online, 24/7. Its parliament and civil courts are entirely paperless, and there is a high level of satisfaction among users in having access to a more efficient, customer-friendly system for day-to-day interactions with a broad range of government benefits and services. This aggressive move to e-government, which is working well in practice, would not be possible without first developing a national sense of digital trust.

The United States must begin to close its own digital trust gap, both for its domestic needs and for its broader ability to have its companies expand into markets abroad where digital trust is required to be globally competitive. According to PwC's 2017 U.S. Consumer Intelligence Series, only 25% of American consumers believe that most companies handle sensitive personal data responsibly. This stark number underscores the lack of confidence that has resulted from data privacy being treated largely as an afterthought once a major data breach occurs.

The more prudent approach would be a long-term focus on building digital trust. Here, there should be a coordinated effort by the private and public sectors, since major aspects of digital life, such as ecommerce and eGovernment, will first depend upon a positive perception of digital trust. Government regulation regarding better consumer notice and consent provisions may be useful, but the uncertainty of whether and when any effective new national laws may be enacted requires voluntary activities to build digital trust, which will take time.

So at the very least, each online company should send its customers a holiday e-card that says "We Take Digital Trust Seriously—Here's How." Within it, the message should articulate what practical steps are being taken to bring these words to life. In doing so, companies will need to look inward regarding their own ability to foster such trust, and assess whether they can do better in creating a digital trust environment that produces enduring loyalty among its customers.

Stuart N. Brotman

How Enhancing Digital Trust and Privacy Protection Can Support a New Arab Spring

The heightened interest in greater digital privacy protection is not just an American phenomenon; there may be a different type of progressive movement emerging in the Arab Middle East. Although the Arab Spring protests of 2010–2012 may now seem like a moment in time, any new comparable movement will need to account for increased anxiety over digital trust in social media and eroding confidence in government regulation to address digital privacy concerns.

Northwestern University in Qatar is one of six American universities that have been operating degree programs in Doha's Education City for more than a decade. Since 2013, a research team there has conducted a landmark annual survey of seven countries—Egypt, Jordan, Tunisia, Saudi Arabia, Qatar, the United Arab Emirates (UAE), and Lebanon. This region is now back in the global headlines after the successful U.S. drone strike in Iraq of Iranian Major General Qassim Suleimani, particularly regarding what level of geopolitical destabilization in the region may follow.

Unlike the Arab Spring that began nearly a decade ago, when social media in the region was instrumental as a mobilization tool but still in its infancy, there now are social media influencers in these countries that can enhance citizen mobilization efforts. This is significant because these influencers can supplement, and in some cases, displace, the tightly held news media controls that are prevalent in the Arab Middle East. This development can be helpful to the United States as it seeks a more direct link to nationals in these countries who otherwise might be inundated with anti-American reporting by state-controlled mass media.

Social media followers of these influencers now exceed those who check their email or play games online. Yet nationals in these countries also are wary of the news they get on social media, with only the Saudis and the Emiratis reflecting a significant sense of increased trust in these news sources.

One reason for this dissonance—relying on social media more while trusting its credibility less—may be due to a growing concern about online surveillance, with nationals in all countries except Qatar showing a sizable increase in apprehension. On average, about half of Internet users in the seven surveyed countries worry about companies using their personal information without their consent. In Saudi Arabia and Tunisia, there also is a growing fear of government surveillance. And in Egypt, the researchers were prohibited from even asking about this. Enough said.

Between 2017 and 2019, all the surveyed countries except Qatar showed an increase in the desire to have tighter government regulation of digital privacy put in place: 2/3 of nationals in the surveyed countries now indicate that the Internet should be more tightly regulated to protect user privacy. Such regulation, however, also can mean tighter control over what users are able to access online, including news that their country may not want them to know about. This would be counterproductive to those envisioning a new Arab Spring, since it would signal tighter control over social media along with mass media.

This can create doubt about any comprehensive government solution to quell online privacy fears, leading to changing digital behaviors that can help alleviate such concerns without enabling governments to inject more content control as a part of the policy bargain. With the exception of Egypt (an outlier again), the difference between 2017 and 2019 has been dramatic.

During this time frame, 40% of citizens in these countries have changed their privacy settings, 30% post less often and share less sensitive information, and 20% have stopped using some social media or have begun using pseudonyms on certain online platforms. They have migrated to WhatsApp for its privacy protecting capabilities, and away from Facebook, Twitter, Instagram, and Snapchat. Virtual Private Networks (VPNs) also have become more prevalent in several countries due to their greater privacy protections. In the UAE, however, VPN use is illegal, which may tamp down confidence that government privacy regulation would be in the best interests of consumers. And not surprisingly, the researchers were not even allowed to ask about this possibility in Egypt.

For those who believe that an Arab Spring resurgence still is possible, it is heartening to note that social media now is achieving greater parity in reach with state-controlled media. This may be helpful as nationals in the seven surveyed countries increasingly look to social media influencers as essential digital figures who help them learn and interpret the fast-breaking news about developments in the region. And for privacy protection, they are discovering that self-help is possible, too.

The United States and its Western allies now have an opportunity to support a new and different Arab Spring. An important aspect will be their activities to help build trust for these influencers, provide better technologies for privacy protection, and enable more fact-based journalism that offers a nuanced context for rapidly shifting events in the Arab Middle East. These strategic confidence measures can help reignite the flame of democratic values that has dimmed over time.

Why Data Portability
Promotes Competition

When fifty-one leading CEOs recently sent a letter to congressional leaders to urge the adoption of a national consumer data privacy law, they indicated that one reason for its enactment would be to "enable continued innovation and growth in the data economy." Now, a focused bipartisan Senate bill has emerged that promises to support greater innovation through stimulating competition among Internet platform providers. It has a clunky name—Augmenting Capability and Competition by Enabling Service Switching—that allows it to use the acronym "ACCESS," but that's probably the only part that should be overlooked.

The core of the legislation, introduced by Senators Mark Warner (D-VA), Richard Blumenthal (D-CT) and Josh Hawley (R-MO), would be a federal requirement that every major tech platform (i.e., with over 100 million monthly users) must offer consumers the ability to transfer their personal data to a competing provider, utilizing a structured, commonly used, machine-readable format. That ability exists today throughout the European Union, in Canada and Mexico, and even in Saudi Arabia. In effect, this would mean that if you wanted to move from Gmail to Hotmail, or from Facebook to LinkedIn, the process would be relatively seamless, based on a user request to transfer data from one account to another.

This has obvious benefits for consumers, who would not be locked into a particular platform service due to having important data that reside there. But equally important, this would provide a competitive spur for companies, allowing better offerings of privacy-enhancing features that would help to retain existing users and attract new ones.

This type of system would work. November 201 marked the 16th anniversary since the Federal Communications Commission ("FCC") required number portability for all landline and wireless telephone providers, which allows consumers to leave their service painlessly for another in the same geographic area. Simply put, if you like your number, you can keep it.

Competition here has proven to be a powerful economic regulator, as customers can switch services freely when a more attractive deal, such as unlimited data or a better family plan, comes along. For data portability, a similar competitive environment can take hold; companies may begin offering enhanced privacy protection if there is an economic penalty at risk in the form of fewer customers and reduced advertising revenue.

There are technical issues at play in data portability, and these should not be underestimated. Platform services have not been designed with this capability, and they would need to make appropriate adjustments to enable handing off large amounts of personalized data to another provider, securely and without error. But they are not about to initiate such a sea change without a legal requirement that they do so.

Legislation could accomplish this, but there may be a quicker, more effective way to achieve a comparable outcome. The FCC, which developed the mandatory number portability regime for telephones, could initiate a rulemaking proceeding to extend this policy framework to Internet platform services.

Although the FCC does not have direct regulatory authority over Facebook, Google, and their peers, the agency has power to regulate the practices of Internet Service Providers ("ISPs"), which are the gateways for platform services. ISPs thus are in a strong position to facilitate the offering of data portability by platform services. Under this scenario, the FCC could develop a regulation that all ISPs enable this, with the costs of data transfer to be borne by the platform services, not the ISPs or consumers. This would promote competition among platform service providers. Some phase in period also would be necessary to enable the development of technical standards for data transfer and testing.

The FCC has already managed number portability successfully, and the ISPs have deep technical capability that could be leveraged by platform services as they move to comply with this new requirement. Given the uncertainty of having the ACCESS Act passed during this Congress, there is no reason to have such a good idea linger without a practical implementation alternative.

In an economy driven by the holy grail of competition, which the letter-writing CEOs extolled, data portability is premised on accepted business principles, common sense, and good social policy, rather than on government overreach.

The linkage between consumer privacy protection and continued digital innovation in the digital economy now faces a reality check. Data portability is Exhibit A for whether competition rhetoric can be translated into a tangible plan that benefits consumers and businesses alike.

Low-Income Citizens Deserve
Better Digital Privacy Protection Too

When the Federal Communications Commission began its Lifeline program 35 years ago, the nation was dominated by landline telephones and had no commercial Internet service. And smartphones seemed like something that appeared on the futuristic cartoon series, *The Jetsons*.

In these simpler times, there was all upside and no downside to the Lifeline program. Typically, it would provide a significant monthly discount for eligible low-income subscribers, with a limit of one discount per household. Since its inception, the Lifeline program has been available to those who are at or below 135% of the Federal Policy Guidelines for income, or those in federal assistance programs such as the Supplemental Nutrition Assistance Program or Medicaid. Its geographic reach is expansive, covering all states, U.S. territories and tribal lands.

The program has been extremely beneficial in providing a vital communications link to friends, family, employers, and social services. In 2016, the FCC enacted a much-needed comprehensive reform and modernization of the Lifeline program. Notably, Lifeline now includes broadband Internet as well as conventional voice service, whether offered via a wire or wirelessly. The Lifeline budget for the subsidy is administered federally, but the providers of Lifeline services—the telecommunication companies that customers interface with—

are overseen by individual states and territories, which also provide general consumer protection for their residents.

A number of companies compete for the ability to offer Lifeline service, often providing a free or reduced-cost smartphone as part of the package. This phone has both cellular telephone and Wi-Fi capability, and comes with preloaded apps. It also has limits on the amount of talk, text, and data that Lifeline customers will receive under their discounted plan.

This is where the good news about such a useful government program begins to grow darker. According to Malwarebytes Labs senior malware intelligence analyst Nathan Collier, at least one such carrier—Assurance Wireless by Virgin Mobile—is offering a $35 smartphone that has preinstalled apps to collect user data, create backdoors for future access, and enable auto-installers for other apps. These activities are undertaken without any customer knowledge or consent, while providing a potential for malware to be installed later on when an app update becomes available.

In short, consumer privacy is being compromised by virtue of a smartphone being offered as part of the federal Lifeline program. Only the most sophisticated technical users will even know how to remove these apps that they did not agree to have downloaded at all.

Here's how this can be stopped: since it is connected to the Lifeline program, the FCC could prohibit any company from offering free or reduced-cost smartphones that come with preinstalled apps. It should require that Lifeline customers be provided information about why an app would be useful, along with an opportunity to choose whether to download it or not.

Additionally, carriers should be required to report to the FCC how they screen apps at the outset and in updates, including disclosure of what user information is being collected and how it is being used. Customers should also have access to this disclosure so that any consent given is informed consent.

Granted, this FCC regulation, while feasible, may take time to be enacted in light of the agency's lengthy procedural rules. In the interim, as well as after the FCC acts, states and territories have existing consumer protection authority to pursue specific carriers that are enabling potential privacy-harming malware in apps that are provided to unsuspecting customers when they turn on their smartphones. This need for consumer protection is even more pronounced since it involves a federal subsidy program that has such a salutary purpose.

It's bad public policy for federal dollars to be used to undermine digital privacy in this way, and the practice needs no new law to be enacted by Congress in order for it to end. A well-known part of the medical Hippocratic oath—"do no harm"—should apply to the Lifeline program, the sooner the better.

Stuart N. Brotman

Smart Cities Require
Better Digital Privacy Planning

We've moved beyond the initial excitement about the sizzle of smart cities. The basic idea—much heralded but limited so far in practical application—is to create a digital mobility ecosystem in a dense urban center. Its components would include a modernized electric grid (ideally powered by renewable energy sources), extensive availability of mass transit and electric vehicle chargers, and state-of-the-art traffic controls that are based on real-time commuting and pedestrian patterns. As Columbus, Ohio, the first winner of the U.S. Department of Transportation's Smart City Challenge, notes, "As a region with urban sprawl, we are committed to a new, improved ecosystem to move people and goods."

The distance between concept and proof of concept remains significant, however, particularly since there is little government funding at any level for anything more than a series of test beds (Columbus only has $50 million in public and private funding to date, for example). While smart city projects are useful in generating essential technical knowledge, they are not being designed to capture critical behavioral insights that will affect how city residents (and taxpayers) will utilize and support any initiative to make their city "smart."

This means that it won't be enough for cities to roll out ambitious plans, accompanied by a splashy video and a striking website, that deliver more heat than light to businesses and the public alike. That's because the development of a smart city model will involve capturing, disseminating, and storing massive amounts of data that is available on a 24/7 basis. Some will be aggregated data that preserve individual anonymity, but anything that involves individual or household usage (e.g., energy management monitoring) will by necessity require personally identifiable information.

Here's how those who are thinking about digital privacy in a smart city context might approach this elephant in the room— gingerly, of course. First, digital privacy needs to be viewed in political terms along with the technical requirements that will enable a smart city ecosystem. Since virtually everyone in a city is a stakeholder, this raises issues about how to solicit input, and comply with legal requirements for doing so, from businesses, community groups, and individuals regarding their expectations for smart city digital privacy protection.

A diverse digital privacy task force should be organized at the earliest possible opportunity by the municipal authority charged with smart city planning. It should report to the mayor, with written reports issued at least on a quarterly basis for public comment. Anything less runs the risk of raising community ire for insufficient transparency and accountability.

Cities also need to understand better the economics of digital privacy protection, particularly as they begin to draft Requests for Proposals (RFPs) from private sector vendors. Absent this analysis, these RFPs may yield too many bidders that ultimately will not be able to deliver under a fixed-price contract.

Smart city planning also needs to have as wide a technological view as possible. For example, it should compare fiber optic backbone networking capability with emerging 5G networks that may be more efficient on balance. And since biometric data gathering increasingly will be used in smart cities on a massive scale, it should be added to the cost-benefit trade-offs that will need to be considered.

Accounting for digital privacy concerns to a complex set of smart city planning considerations may be too much for some municipalities. In reaction, they may impose reflexive moratoriums on certain capabilities, such as facial recognition, or pull back on their ambitious plans in part or in whole.

This points to the need for more collective knowledge regarding benchmarks and best practices that cities should share with their population size and demographic peers. Here, the United States Conference of Mayors, representing over 1100 cities with populations of 300,000 or more, is well positioned to facilitate robust information sharing about smart city digital privacy policies. Otherwise, a proprietary sense of smart city planning will create urban silos that are not part of a beneficial national movement. Smart cities need scale, and the more they are able to learn from others, the better positioned they will be both internally and as contributors to a larger nationwide aspiration.

Perhaps the best advice about how to make smart city planning smarter in the area of digital privacy was provided in another context by the leader who understood how important it was to establish an interstate highway system in the 1950s to physically move people and goods throughout the United States. "If a problem cannot be solved, enlarge it," counseled Dwight D. Eisenhower. Digital privacy is one concern where enlargement will underscore its importance, while also increasing the likelihood of long-term smart city success.

Why Broadband Network Expansion
Must Consider Digital Privacy Protection

March 2020 marked the ten-year anniversary of the National Broadband Plan's release. This plan was mandated by the bipartisan passage of the American Recovery and Reinvestment Act of 2009. The Federal Communications Commission (FCC) was vested by Congress to oversee the report, with significant input from the White House and a broad range of executive branch and independent regulatory agencies. In particular, the plan was developed to ensure that every American has "access to broadband capability."

Although the growth of high-speed broadband networks has been impressive in the ensuing decade, the FCC estimates that 21 million Americans still lack broadband. What was once viewed primarily as a federal policymaking responsibility to enhance broadband availability, however, now is being passed on to individual states that are better able to deal with their local situations.

Regardless of who leads the charge, a key aspect of the National Broadband Plan remains unfulfilled. As the Pew Research Center recently noted, "Communities without reliable high-speed internet service cite a growing gap between the resources and opportunities available to their residents and those in communities that have a robust network. Recognizing the importance of broadband responding to such frustrations, states are seeking to close this gap. Most have established programs to expand broadband to communities that lack it or are underserved."

The plan recognized that many users are increasingly concerned about their lack of control over sensitive personal data. That certainly has not decreased over time, particularly as more of these data are collected, stored, and disseminated to third parties, often without the knowledge or consent of individual consumers. But it did not address how the legal landscape should be reformed. In part, this explains the flurry of congressional and state legislative interest that now is in motion, especially since the enactment of the EU's General Data Protection Regulation and the California Consumer Privacy Act.

So the plan is interesting to review today not just in terms of numerical benchmarks for broadband expansion or for what gaps in rural areas need to be closed when marketplace forces are unlikely to do so on their own. Renewed focus should be devoted to the plan's three central questions aimed at clarifying the existing patchwork of potentially confusing privacy regulations. First, what obligations do firms that collect, analyze, or monetize personal data or create digital profiles of individuals have to consumers in terms of data sharing, collection, storage, safeguarding and accountability? Second, what, if any, new obligations should firms have to transparently disclose their use of, access to, and retention of personal data? Third, how can informed consent principles be applied to personal data usage and disclosures?

These remain central issues that all policy makers still need to address. That's because, as the plan notes, increased privacy protection could address "digital interaction and seamless content sharing" that could "drive more Americans online, increase the utilization of the Internet and help American businesses and organizations develop deeper and more trusted relationships with their customers and clients."

One specific set of privacy recommendation deserves closer attention in this regard. The plan called for spurring development of trusted "identity providers" to assist consumers in managing their data in a manner that maximizes the privacy and security of their information. Standard safe harbor provisions in legislation could allow companies to be acknowledged as trusted intermediaries that properly safeguard information, following appropriately strict guidelines and audits on data protection and privacy. And the plan also called for the creation of a legislative program that provides insurance to these trusted intermediaries.

Viewed with the passage of time, it's clear that increasing the number of Americans who have broadband network availability at home remains a worthy goal. But it needs to be pursued within a larger context that links network expansion with enhanced digital privacy protection. As the plan wisely noted then—which is equally applicable today—"Broadband networks only create value to consumers and businesses when they are used in conjunction with broadband-capable devices to deliver useful applications and content." The long-term health of our nation's broadband ecosystem surely will require more holistic thinking about the linkage between broadband network expansion and digital privacy protection, too.

Stuart N. Brotman

The Case for
a Federal Digital Privacy Strike Force

With the recent enactment of the first-ever federal privacy
legislation dealing with robocalls—the Telephone Robocall
Abuse Criminal Enforcement and Deterrence Act (TRACED)—
there has already been notable activity at various executive
branch and independent regulatory agencies. In late January, the
Department of Justice filed lawsuits seeking temporary
restraining orders against five companies and three individuals,
based on allegations that they had carried hundreds of millions
of fraudulent robocalls to American consumers. Within days, the
Federal Trade Commission (FTC) sent letters to 19 Voice over
Internet Protocol (VOIP) providers to warn them that any
assistance or facilitation of telemarketing through robocalls
would be deemed to violate the new law. And less than a week
later after that, the Federal Communications Commission (FCC)
sent letters to seven U.S. telephone companies that provide
gateway service for international robocalls into stateside
networks. It asked for these companies to cooperate in tracing
back these calls to help the FCC pursue enforcement actions that
are warranted under the TRACED Act.

Despite the close timing of these separate actions, the three
agencies were not acting in an explicitly coordinated manner to
protect the privacy of individuals who are bombarded with
unwanted robocalls at all hours of the day and night. But there is
an existing framework that can be established in short order to

ensure greater efficiency and effectiveness in enforcing the TRACED Act. It's called a Strike Force.

Last November, for example, the Department of Justice (DOJ) formed the Procurement Collusion Strike Force to focus on deterring, investigating, and prosecuting antitrust crimes that undermine competition in government procurement, grant and program funding. This Strike Force has several internal DOJ divisions that will be working closely together, including the Antitrust Division and thirteen U.S. Attorneys offices. The FBI also will be involved, along with the Department of Defense Office of Inspector General, the U.S. Postal Service Office of Inspector General, and other federal offices of inspector generals.

The organization of such an entity, operating continuously with buy-in from the leadership of its constituent units, sends a powerful message that these agencies are willing and able to pursue bad actors that are involved in government procurement misdeeds. It also marshals resources to minimize duplicative efforts that can be costly to taxpayers and be less impactful in achieving desirable outcomes.

Other older Strike Forces have been established using this cross-agency collaborative approach, and seem to be working well. A notable success is the Health Care Strike Force that brings together the investigative and analytical resources of the DOJ, the FBI, the Department of Health and Human Services, the Drug Enforcement Administration, the Centers for Medicare and Medicaid Services, the Internal Revenue Service, and other government agencies. Those in the Strike Force work full time on the cases focused on health care fraud that results in patient harm and/or large financial losses to the public treasury. This enables a high level of coordinated expertise that can be brought to bear.

That brings us back to enhancing current digital privacy protection. Even without any new federal privacy legislation, which is unlikely to be enacted before the 2020 elections, there already are a number of privacy laws in place that could benefit from the coordinated Strike Force model. In addition to the

TRACED Act, these include privacy protections in the Communications Act that are applicable to video and telephony services, the Financial Modernization Act's financial data safeguards, and the Electronic Communications Privacy Act's wiretap, stored communication, and computer fraud/abuse provisions. With the enhanced resources of a Strike Force, these laws could be enforced more often and more vigorously, creating greater digital privacy protection through improved interagency coordination.

In the longer term, this Digital Privacy Strike Force then could be deployed if and when broader measures are established through any new law. The Department of Justice, the FTC, and the FCC all will continue to play a role in this area. By acting in concert now, they will be well prepared to undertake an expanded set of challenges that any future legislation might create.

Stuart N. Brotman

Why Hacking Must be Addressed in Digital Privacy Policymaking

Digital privacy is one side of a two-sided policy coin. Virtually all attention to date has been focused on developing legal and regulatory remedies to address this pervasive public concern. But in doing so, they have devoted little attention to the flip side—namely, digital hacking. Although data systems that are thought to be secure from intrusion can be subject to random technological breakdowns or human error, there usually are far less benign explanations for major cybersecurity breaches that expose personal information on a massive scale.

This reality should make *Why Hackers Win* by Patrick Burkart and Tom McCourt (University of California Press, 2019) essential reading for those grappling with how best to craft a workable framework for enhancing digital privacy protection. Burkart is a professor at Texas A&M's Department of Communication, and McCourt is a professor at Fordham University's Department of Communication and Media Studies.

The authors describe hacking as "an interface between technical code (the structure of trusted systems), legal code (the laws that govern their access and use), and social code (their impact on society, particularly in terms of privacy and sanctioned activity)." And they discount a popular but erroneous perception that hacking is an activity typically undertaken by a lone wolf operating in an offshore bedroom or basement. Rather, the authors contend that "[a]lthough hacking ostensibly undermines their own security, corporations and states paradoxically use hacking for gain. Hacking can suit a broad spectrum of purposes, including gathering intelligence, managing crises, and accumulating competitive advantage over rivals."

They also note that while examining abuses of power through exploiting computer vulnerabilities, they did not find "master conspiracies" of surveillance and espionage, or even a systematic imposition of will, in coordinated hacking campaigns. Instead, they see "a proliferation of agents contributing to offenses and defenses played in long games and embedded in global networks." Soberly, they assert that hacking has become "a mundane, 'business as usual' application of force for many enterprises."

Their research includes notable real-world examples of hacking undertaken for strategic political and economic ends. Including the disruption of the SWIFT international payments system, the Paradise Papers (13.4 million confidential documents relating to offshore investments that were leaked to two German reporters), and the ways in which states have targeted journalists and dissidents through hacking. They also discuss "growth hacks" by companies such as Uber, News Corp., and Volkswagen, which is the rapid accumulation of user metrics to achieve short-term growth through low-cost marketing techniques. Such activities, while privacy invasive, have "increasingly become a standard business strategy." In short, "hacking and cybersecurity reinforces and accelerates each other in social, economic and political life."

As with those who advocate greater transparency for digital data collection, storage, and dissemination activities, the hacking universe, including cybersecurity defenses, also needs greater exposure: "The torrents of public money flowing into private security operations," argue the authors, "should be accounted for and audited by elected representatives. Debates about the social value of these expenditures than can be raised."

And the United States would be well served by establishing a counterpart to Canada's Citizens Lab at the University of Toronto, which examines samples of spyware and other forms of invasive software that is submitted by other researchers or individuals who suspect that they have been targeted. As Burkart and McCourt note, the Citizens Lab "provides a model for opening up, rather than enclosing and privatizing, actionable knowledge about real-time threats to the public network and their indicators. These disclosures can undermine the secrecy that preserves the advantages of spyware vendors who hoard vulnerabilities." These two measures—public auditing of private cybersecurity firms and public funding for a national facility that can test and expose system vulnerabilities—represent tangible steps that Congress can take to help address the other side of the proverbial privacy policy coin.

It will not be enough to explain why hackers win. Those who are developing an activist agenda for digital privacy protection must be willing to advance approaches that raise the barriers for hacking at the same time they argue for higher digital privacy protection guardrails to control the behavior of private companies.

Digital Privacy Policy Needs Carrots
to Encourage Innovation

So much of the current discussion about digital privacy policy emphasizes the stick part of a carrot-and-stick approach. The European Union's General Data Protection Regulation (GDPR) and the California Consumer Privacy Act (CCPA), both now in force, emphasize penalties for companies that violate its provisions. EU member countries, for example, already have levied 190 fines and penalties.

Only the GDPR imposes a mandatory, affirmative obligation on organizations covered by it to consider privacy at the initial design stages of developing new products, processes, or services that involve personal data processing. Those found to be in violation can face financial and other penalties imposed by a country's data protection agency. The EU's approach here is salutary. It has developed a policy that privacy protection should be built into digital information technology systems at the outset. But the GDPR is all sticks and no carrots.

The goal of the EU's privacy by design requirement is to encourage innovation in developing, on a continuing basis, new engineering methods that serve the aim of better consumer privacy protection at the outset. Innovation, however, typically is produced in the marketplace rather than by government fiat. The CCPA, in contrast, implicitly recognizes that innovation cannot be required in the manner that the GDPR specifies.

But that leaves open how the United States, whether at a state or federal level, will be encouraging built-in privacy controls—privacy by design—both at the system and device levels, within any new legislative or regulatory framework. In order to do so, it should view innovation as the driving force for this concept, and accordingly begin to explore what carrots it can offer along with potential sticks attached to effective compliance provisions.

The new app Jumbo is a case in point. It manages privacy settings for users on four different services: Twitter, Facebook, Google search, and Amazon's Alexa, with future plans to also include Instagram and Tinder. The app is only available now on iPhones, however the company says an Android version is forthcoming.

Viewed in a broader context, Jumbo represents just the type of privacy innovation that should be encouraged, rather than reduced to a regulatory compliance checklist. This means that U.S. policymakers have an opportunity to think about innovation carrots as well as sticks, which the GDPR and the CCPA so far have failed to do. There are a range of incentives that might stimulate more, better, and broader privacy by design innovation, such as targeted R&D tax credits; limited antitrust immunity for companies in the same field that want to jointly engage in privacy by design; or voluntary safe harbor provisions that would help reduce regulatory liability.

The United States is the beacon of the world in encouraging innovation. Creative and proactive policymaking can reward innovators as well as punish those who are lax in staying within legally defined digital privacy parameters. Our nation now should see how to adapt a carrot-rich approach to privacy by design, which can complement the need to utilize sticks in order to enhance current consumer digital privacy protection.

Why You Need to Know
What the Government Does with Your Data

Privacy and cybersecurity are two sides of the same coin. When a government agency asks individuals to provide personally identifiable information, many may be comfortable doing so. But if those individuals learn that information may be shared with third parties, such as government contractors, who may use it in wholly unintended ways, they likely would feel far less comfortable sharing that information. And if the third-party data storage system is hacked, the breach can raise serious cybersecurity concerns, both for the integrity of the system and the privacy of the individuals whose information has been obtained by bad actors.

This chain reaction begins at the government level—whether federal, state, or local. Government agencies have the highest obligation to provide transparency to the public regarding the personally identifiable information, or PII, they provide to contractors, for what purpose, and with what level of confidence that the contractor has a robust cybersecurity system in place to prevent unauthorized internal and external access. Yet today, once people submit data to complete a government application, there is little if any notice regarding how an agency will provide that information to others. There may be valid reasons for such third-party access, but at a minimum, agencies should be legally obligated to disclose this at the time such information is requested.

Senator Maggie Hassan (D-NH) is spot on in her recent letter requesting that the Government Accountability Office review Homeland Security Department policies regarding how the department shares PII with government contractors. As a member of the Senate Homeland Security and Governmental Affairs Committee, she said it is essential that DHS "protect PII that is collected on the department's behalf from improper access or use." Her letter cited three data breaches of DHS contractors over the past year, including the theft of photos of travelers at the border from a Customs and Border Protection contractor.

Hassan's inquiry has broader implications. Lawmakers should request that GAO conduct a governmentwide review of how departments and agencies share PII, to develop a comprehensive understanding of how contractors are using these data. Beyond Washington, state and city legislators also should be making similar requests for the same purpose.

With so much attention focused on how Big Tech is using PII on a massive scale, it's timely to extend this to the public sector, particularly since the PII it requests often is needed for valid operational purposes. The possibility that government contractors may obtain this information, only to have it compromised or stolen due to inadequate cybersecurity measures, is real. It poses an imminent threat, and we lack appropriate measures to limit the transmittal of government-gathered PII, and to protect it once a contractor has access.

Agencies need to clarify their policies and share that information with the public. Those are critical next steps needed to address this serious privacy and cybersecurity challenge.

California's New Privacy Law
Should Apply to the Government, Too

The clock is ticking on the reality of the California Consumer Privacy Act (CCPA), which took effect on January 1, 2020. As a practical matter, it still will await enforcement rules to be drafted by Attorney General Xavier Becerra's office to meet a statutory July 1, 2020 deadline. Two of the CCPA's important principles are minimization (narrowly tailoring data to its authorized use) and sharing limits (clear rules to limit data sharing with service providers and third parties to that which is needed to carry out the express purposes expected and authorized by consumers).

It will be interesting to see how these principles are applied to California state and municipal agencies. Although many perceive the CCPA as a potent weapon to be used against private sector firms, this should not obscure that bad behavior also is possible by government itself. This may be even more egregious since consumers will have a difficult time opting out of obtaining government permissions or benefits that only can be provided by government.

The California Department of Motor Vehicles collects massive amounts of personal data to process driver's licenses and registrations. The information it gathers also is especially useful outside DMV to law enforcement authorities who enforce traffic and vehicular violations, as well as in broader aspects of crime prevention. These valid and varied purposes justify why so much data is gathered, stored and shared internally and with other state and local agencies. Presumably, the DMV also has developed its own plan for data minimization and sharing limits.

But to date, this plan is opaque to the public, with the same pattern extending across hundreds of state government agencies and thousands of local ones. Alas, the CCPA's broad coverage in these areas applies to businesses but not to any level of government. And regardless of the public visibility of government agency minimization and data sharing limit plans, government agencies will not be restricted under the CCPA in making third-party access to sensitive personal information available on a commercial basis.

The DMV, for example, is doing just that to bring additional revenue into its coffers—over $50 million annually for names, physical addresses, and car registration information, according to Motherboard Tech by Vice. It has been doing so for at least six years, too, with eager buyers such as data broker LexisNexis and consumer credit reporting agency Experian, along with garden-variety private investigators developing leads for domestic dispute files. Consequently, state agencies will not be legally obligated to disclose this practice, nor will they be prohibited from selling this information to outsiders with very different needs for the data, or even without any public purpose.

The CCPA specifies that private companies operating websites must include a "Do Not Sell My Personal Information" option on their home pages. Voluntary government compliance with this requirement is possible, but highly unlikely. Alternatively, the law could be extended to cover the DMV with this requirement, with a comparable mandate for those applying or renewing at a local office. It could cover all state and local government agencies, too, for both online and in-person transactions. The next iteration of the CCPA already has begun, so this seems to be an appropriate legislative route.

Since the CCPA amendment process is complex and not a sure bet, however, the simpler and more timely solution would be an executive order issued by Gov. Gavin Newsom that either prohibits unrelated third-party sale of personal information by government agencies, or allows it provided that consumers are notified and can opt out easily through a one-click process online or a check mark on a paper form.

Data privacy principles are nice to hear about, but are only meaningful if they apply to businesses and government alike, since sensitive personal information is the same regardless of who is collecting, storing, and disseminating it.

Stuart N. Brotman

Why a Federal Revenge Porn Law is Needed

The resignation of U.S. Rep. Katie Hill, a Democrat from California, has attracted global headlines focusing on her private sexual relations with her estranged husband and an "inappropriate" relationship with a campaign aide. The online posting of nude photos of Hill and a female campaign aide led the House Ethics Committee to initiate a formal investigation. That proceeding now is moot due to Hill's resignation. POLITICO reported that "colleagues were uniformly shocked and saddened by the collapse of the freshman star's political career."

Yet on Capitol Hill, where there is much ongoing discussion about developing digital privacy legislation that would establish greater legal liability for Big Tech. There is little talk about the linkage between privacy and the nonconsensual posting of these types of photos, which is often referred to as "revenge porn."

Although most states and the District of Columbia have enacted some type of criminal penalty for this activity—ranging from a misdemeanor to a felony, with possible jail time and fines often included as well —they represent a patchwork quilt of laws that focus more on the harm of displaying sexual images than on the violation of personal privacy that this act really represents.

Only a handful of states, including Delaware, Georgia, and Hawaii, explicitly recognize the core privacy invasion aspect of revenge porn. Consequently, a victim may have little civil recourse to recover monetary damages under a specific state law. Hill's remedy may depend on the state where the photos were taken or uploaded, even though they were distributed nationwide and beyond.

Hill has retained counsel to pursue litigation against anyone who leaked these photos without her permission. Presumably, the next step will be filing a lawsuit based on a state's revenge porn law. But since there is no federal revenge porn law in place, there are gaps, because not all states have enacted laws covering it (some also cover only minors, which would exclude the 32-year-old Hill), and in any case the penalties may vary widely.

Although Hill's damaging disclosures about her romantic life created an avalanche of publicity and political liability, they also underscore that congressional policymakers now have an opportunity to reflect their privacy concerns in a timely and concrete way—namely, by enacting a federal revenge porn law covering victims of all ages throughout the United States, and one that enables both criminal punishment and civil damage awards. If this results in legislative action, perhaps it will carry with it the name of someone who otherwise may be remembered as a blip in the 24/7 news cycle—Katie Hill's Law.

How Public Libraries Can Help
Close America's Digital Privacy Divide

This year's Academy Awards were presented against the backdrop of a recent Gallup Poll that shows Americans actually prefer going to a library over going to a movie theater, by a lot. The poll for 2019 activity indicated that survey respondents listed library attendance at the top, with 10.5 average visits a year. In contrast, going to a movie at a movie theater was roughly half that amount—5.3 average visits a year.

These data may be disheartening to Hollywood, but they also suggest an enormous role that public libraries in virtually every U.S. community can play in our nation's quest for better privacy protection.

Today's public libraries have broadened their role significantly beyond circulating books and being available to assist with reference activities. As vital 21ˢᵗ century institutions with continuous public funding, libraries serve as an essential center of equal opportunities for everyone to education and culture.

They are usually well equipped with high-performance computers and fast broadband connections, enabling Internet access for anyone who comes in; additionally, they are expanding their collections of digital print and audiovisual materials dramatically, which enables widespread remote online access to anyone with a library card.

Stuart N. Brotman

At the center of this institutional transformation is a major push, both in terms of programs and personnel, for libraries to promote greater digital literacy. According to the Public Library Association: "Digital literacy initiatives within local libraries are imperative to helping our patrons create and upload resumes, sign up and use email to communicate with friends and family, download an app to get a ride to the airport, create and edit a presentation to share at work, search for a new doctor online, create a movie online to complete a school project, communicate with a computer technician when their device has issues, and so much more. The minutiae of digital literacy needs are endless and they continue to expand over time."

The American Library Association reports that nearly 90% of libraries offer digital literacy training. Yet such training only is offered by less than 60% of libraries in safe online practices and social media use.

This represents what I would term as a "digital privacy divide." There now should be a major national effort to enhance teaching digital privacy protection as part of any digital literacy initiative in a public library.

These libraries reach an expansive segment of the population across all age and demographic categories. This makes them very well positioned to offer privacy teaching in digital literacy programs, both in brick-and-mortar locations and via remote online access.

And libraries are especially popular with those in the 18–29 age range, which is dominated by digital natives who may be highly adept technologically, but also less concerned about protecting their digital information. The Gallup Poll shows they exceed the already high average overall numbers for library visits last year.

The public at large would also welcome an initiative for public libraries to help close the digital privacy divide. For example, in the Pew Research Center's 2015 report, "Libraries at the Crossroads," 76% of survey respondents indicated that libraries "definitely" should offer programs to teach people how to protect their privacy and security online.

A separate Pew Research Center study completed in late 2019 also showed that less than half of all survey respondents correctly noted that privacy policies are contracts between websites and users about how those sites will use their data. Less than a quarter of survey respondents correctly noted that private browsing only prevents someone using the same computer from seeing one's online activities.

Taken together, the forces of supply and demand, plus a real digital privacy knowledge gap, comprise a compelling argument for public libraries to more aggressively offer privacy training as part of their digital literacy activities. Their infrastructure and community reach are already in place, so any additional resources needed for this focused effort need only be incremental.

To be successful, public libraries will need to develop effective marketing campaigns to publicize their privacy protection training, as well. Some may even want to condition patrons from obtaining a library card, renewing one, or having access to various library services (e.g., remote online access) on the successful completion of digital privacy training.

This initiative can begin as soon as possible. It's not dependent on the enactment of any comprehensive state or federal privacy legislation, which may not be ratified in the foreseeable future.

And it can create both short-term and long-term positive impacts that result in better privacy protection for broad segments of our population. They surely would welcome it, grateful for libraries to assume a more assertive leadership role in this important ongoing area of public concern.

Stuart N. Brotman

Looking at Facial Recognition Software Through A Wide-Angle Lens

Amazon's facial recognition technology, called Amazon Rekognitition, is a growing part of that tech giant's portfolio. Unlike Amazon Prime or Whole Foods, however, it remains largely removed from public awareness. That may change dramatically in the coming months if Amazon CEO Jeff Bezos has his way.

At a recent Alexa conclave in Seattle, Bezos stated that Amazon's public policy team is working on facial recognition regulations. "It's a perfect example of something that has really positive uses, so you don't want to put the brakes on it. But, at the same time, there's also potential for abuses of that kind of technology, so you want regulations."

Amazon has been marketing the Rekognition software to companies and law enforcement agencies rather than to general consumers. Its customers are provided with the capability to match, in real time, photos and videos of people's faces with other facial images. For example, this may aid police and others in combating crime more quickly. But since the technology is not perfect, it may also create false positives that lead to misidentifications and the creation of new rabbit holes for criminal investigations.

And there are those who will be creeped out by this new form of digital surveillance, especially with its ability to be misused. Bezos recognizes this; his call for federal regulation makes business as well as public policy sense since having clearer regulatory guardrails installed as the technology develops will help create greater confidence among current and potential customers. Currently, they may face financial liability for intentional or negligent misuse of the software, and, at the least, a public relations nightmare, such as when a rogue employee uses it for nefarious purposes.

Amazon has announced that it will be drafting proposed legislation for Congress to consider. This will provide a basis for other stakeholders to react and join in the legislative discussion. But that initiative, like facial recognition software, also has potentially negative implications.

First, only addressing this application would be far too narrow an approach. Facial recognition software is part of a larger technological universe—biometric information—that can be gathered through other techniques, including digital fingerprints and eye scans. Consequently, any proposed legislation should encompass a full range of activities involved in capturing, storing, and sharing biometric information. Notice and written consent provisions are also essential to ensure that there is full transparency to those who are providing this information, whether voluntarily or involuntarily.

Federal legislation also should not preempt the ability of individual municipalities to prohibit the use of biometric information matching software by their government agencies. This decision is highly localized and should not be implemented with a one-size-fits-all approach that removes decisional powers from cities and towns. To date, both San Francisco and Oakland, California have enacted such a ban, and others should not be legally prohibited from doing the same.

Exemptions regarding who is covered by biometric information regulations should also be limited. Any legislation should not contain provisions that undermine requirements for subject consent, secure storage, and timely destruction of biometric identifiers. For example, private companies should not escape legal liability if they assert that the biometric information will be used exclusively for employment, human resources, fraud prevention, or security purposes. They also should be covered even if they do not sell, lease, trade, or profit from the biometric information. They should be held to a higher standard than merely protecting biometric information in the same way that other sensitive information is handled internally.

These more expansive principles deserve timely discussion and buy-in from Amazon and others who are offering biometric information matching systems. Alexa was listening closely to Jeff Bezos's Seattle speech, but so too should all those with a stake in having this new technological frontier develop with appropriate safeguards. The necessary focus should be wide angled at the outset to consider all those affected by biometric screening.

NYC Needs A Better Approach
To Regulating Biometric Data

Cities with widespread use of facial recognition technology are now exploring ways to regulate residential building owners' usage of biometric data. Unfortunately, the nation's largest city is moving too quickly to offer a solution that is practical.

New York City's just-proposed facial recognition and biometric data regulation has a clever acronym, KEYS (Keep Entry to Your home Surveillance-free), but not much else to commend its passage by the City Council. Its major provision would prevent residential building owners from requiring that tenants submit to biometric data screening and confirmation in order to gain access to their homes. They would be relegated to using a metal key to gain entry. This might become the only legal method to be allowed if this bill becomes a law.

The rationale, according to New York City Council member Brad Lander, is that "[n]o one should be required to have their movements tracked just to enter their own home, but that is the reality we are starting to face." Lander's approach may be a solution in search of a problem, but we won't know that without first getting a much better sense of the prevalence and use of biometric data in apartment buildings citywide. To date, there is no reliable information about such usage by landlords, making it difficult if not impossible to offer an objective rationale for a government restriction that may be based on conjecture rather than actual experience.

Additionally, even with a key-only requirement, there still may be gathering of biometric data (including photos and fingerprints). And if someone misplaces or loses a key, presumably they would have to present personally identifiable information, such as a driver's license with a photo, in order to gain temporary apartment access or have a new key made.

The current proposal would cover individual units, so that apartment building lobbies and elevators still could require biometric data for a resident to gain initial access or be transported to the appropriate floor. This would make the key-only requirement largely symbolic, since the biometric data could be collected for other building purposes.

Biometric data may result in erroneous software matches, resulting in a denial of unit access. But overall, such data may have the positive effect of deterring and/or decreasing physical break-ins due to faulty locks. With 24/7 security cameras and video systems already in place in most large apartment buildings—typically required by insurance companies—landlords currently have full-motion capability to track the movements of suspicious individuals. This includes near the entrances to apartment units, where critical evidence of illegal entry can be gathered to enable criminal apprehension and prosecution.

The City Council may still wish to act in this area, but it's best to take a more measured approach at the outset. This could involve, as a condition for building licensing, a requirement that all residential building owners be required to inform the city annually about their biometric information–gathering practices and matching systems (including error rates). How comprehensive are they? How are residents informed about their use? Do residents have an option to elect keyed or keyless entry? How many illegal entries have been accomplished when both systems are available?

This type of mandatory building census would be a more logical first step before the city intervenes to create a new regime that may be unwarranted and/or ineffective. An expansive regulatory solution may generate some initial media buzz and political goodwill, but over time the City Council may find that it acted too hastily and too emotionally.

An evidence-based approach is the obvious alternative that New York City and its peers should focus on now. Any enacted law must be tailored to deal with real-world misuses of biometric information rather than a generalized fear that such misuses are inherent or malicious.

Stuart N. Brotman

Making Sure the Next "Killer App" Is Not a Privacy Killer

The app economy, both at home and abroad, is one of the most remarkable and transformative things in recent years and one that people largely take for granted. Just think, a few years ago it would have been inconceivable that you would turn on your phone, activate the GPS, and have a car driven by a complete stranger take you to your destination, but that's Uber.

What about all of those amazing vacation photos that used to sit idle in boxes until relatives came over? Now you can share them on Instagram with the tap of a finger for all the world to see. What about that snarky joke that occurred to you on your drive into work? You can share that through Twitter for all of your "fans" to hear and share. You can surf the web, trade stocks, manage your money, track your fitness, and more, all through apps on your smart phone. It's so ubiquitous that it is almost a given.

The scale of the app economy in the United States is huge—in 2018 alone, $120 billion in gross annual revenue for app stores was generated, according to the analytics firm App Annie. Deloitte indicated that there were more than 317,000 companies active in mobile app development last year, too. Clearly apps are very big business.

The problem is that while there are untold numbers of honest and aboveboard app developers, there are an equal number (and probably a whole lot more) trying to develop a different type of "killer app"—one that could compromise your phone or device, steal your information, spam you, or use your device as a way to get into more important and secure networks.

Both the Google Play Store and Apple's App Store have rules and vetting processes before the apps are allowed to live on the sites. This is, however, a losing proposition. Nearly every day apps are approved that circumvent the rules, change their behavior after they are uploaded, or poach intellectual property directly or indirectly. And a number of third-party app stores and sites have vastly looser rules, if any at all, to screen apps before they are uploaded.

There are other apps that are just malicious vehicles to access your devices and steal your information. Upon downloading some apps, the program will ask you for permission to nearly every element of your phone, including text messaging, contacts, email, and camera. If you aren't savvy, you'll allow the criminals free access to the most personal of devices.

So what are we to do? We need to build out a digital privacy ecosystem of security whereby products and apps are thoroughly tested and vetted independently before being fielded. What might this look like? We see a highly effective system in place today for electrical products. Underwriters Laboratory vets and certifies massive numbers of products as having met its standards. We need to develop a similar approval label system for apps.

Apple's App Store requires some security reviews, for example, but these also could be expanded to include a privacy and cybersecurity vulnerability report card. If an app doesn't meet the highest standards, it shouldn't be sold on the App Store or in the Google Play Store.

Privacy and security shouldn't be an afterthought, but rather at the core of app design. We can do this in part with the aforementioned independent vetting and report card approaches. We also need to change the mindset of app developers. Long term, we need to bake digital privacy into the educational curriculum of students at all levels, as they go on to develop new apps in schools and beyond.

Unless we get a handle on this situation soon, the next killer app could well be the app that kills your privacy.

Stuart N. Brotman

The Google Antitrust Investigations—
Learning from Germany's Facebook Inquiry

In a time of intense political polarization, the news that forty-eight states (all except Alabama and California), along with Puerto Rico and Washington, D.C., have opened antitrust investigations into Google deserves the reporting prominence that it has triggered to date.

The core issue is whether Google is limiting competition in online advertising and the advertising choices for online advertisers, given its dominance as a web search engine. These unprecedented probes add investigative firepower to a comparable federal antitrust inquiry being conducted by the Department of Justice.

After headlines recede, however, these various government antitrust enforcers may find they are legally constrained in seeking an antitrust law remedy that punishes Google for its alleged anticompetitive practices.

That's because Google's behavior may not actually fall within the boundaries of antitrust law at either the state or federal levels. U.S. prosecutors would be well advised to review a recent, largely obscure decision issued by the Higher Regional Court of Düsseldorf to see how facts may ultimately not support actual legal penalties. And they should have their German-English dictionaries handy, or rely (ironically) on a Google Chrome translation, since the court's opinion remains in its native language.

Stuart N. Brotman

The German court was reviewing a similar antitrust investigation of Facebook under that country's antitrust law. The Bundeskartellamt, Germany's competition authority, began its Facebook investigation in March 2016. One piece of advice for U.S. antitrust enforcers of all stripes is that they need to review Google's business model broadly and deeply—as it is now and how it is evolving.

To its credit, the Bundeskartellamt spent several years researching online platforms before it even began its investigation; it is unclear whether this level of necessary pre-investigation research has already taken place in the United States. If not, the initial investigatory steps will need to be directed at gaining a comprehensive understanding of Google's complex and highly profitable business model, which extends well beyond search to email (Gmail) and video (YouTube), for example.

Antitrust law requires an abuse of a dominant position in a market to create an environment that deters competition. Since Google's most prominent online services are free, any anticompetitive effects are unlikely to reach a typical antitrust law benchmark—namely, whether a company is using its dominant position to squeeze out others and increase its prices in the marketplace.

At the consumer level, this may make it difficult for U.S. antitrust enforcers to focus on Google's massive and constant acquisition of data by consumers, including what privacy protections Google is offering users to obtain such valuable data. As the Bundeskartellamt noted, "users have to expect a certain processing of their data if they use such a free service."

Instead, the investigations are more likely to examine how Google merges this consumer data with other data generated by affiliated business units and by third-party websites. In the German case, the concern centered on data collected by services owned by Facebook, such as WhatsApp and Instagram, combined with data from third-party sources that used Facebook's application programming interface (API).

When users visited websites with embedded API, their data were transmitted to Facebook without even pressing a like or share button. In turn, these data were used to target advertisers and generate billions of dollars of revenue.

The Bundeskartellamt, unable to base a theory of consumer harm on a free service, instead argued that this exploitative behavior was unfair to both sides of Facebook's two-sided business model. For the consumer side, it found that "the damage for users lies in the loss of control: they are no longer able to control how their personal data are used."

And for the advertising part of the business model, this aggregation of consumer data made it indispensable—creating a "potential for competitive harm on the side of advertising customers who are faced with a dominant supplier of advertising space."

That brings us to the recent German court review of the Bundeskartellamt investigation. It found that consumers were not harmed by Facebook, which had informed them about data use practices in a lengthy terms of service agreement when they registered as users: "There is no evidence that Facebook obtains the consent of users through coercion, pressure, exploitation of lack of willpower or otherwise unfair means." The court further found that "whether the users act out of indifference or because they do not want to spend the necessary time and effort ... does not matter. Their decision to sign on is ultimately free, uninfluenced and autonomous." And regarding online advertisers, the court ruled that there only could be anticompetitive effects when the ability of Facebook rivals, and their incentives to compete, are diminished: "Not every economic disadvantage inflicted on another company constitutes a hindrance in the antitrust sense," the court said. "What is needed is an impairment of the competitive and entrepreneurial options for action and decision-making."

The court rejected the notion that additional data increase the barriers to competitive entry, and indicated that this issue "requires closer examination and a detailed explanation/review and conclusive presentation by the antitrust authorities."

The Bundeskartellamt bore the burden of proof in the Facebook case, and the court found it failed to show that Facebook was abusing its power by advantageously using aggregated data that no other competitor could generate. In other words, the asymmetry of information may have created a market failure, but that did not justify a conclusion that Facebook exercised illegal market power to harm advertisers through higher pricing.

The torrent of U.S. Google investigations will be extensive and will take several years at a minimum, not counting any possible judicial appeals that may follow. Although the two digital giants are different, they are obvious targets of continuing scrutiny, with antitrust law as one powerful government tool to employ against them.

Several interesting aspects of the German case should be noted in the United States. There may be a significant gap between theories of consumer and advertiser harm that are developed at the outset and Google's actual business model, which continues to change over time. That's why it will be essential for antitrust enforcers to gain an intensive understanding of that model at the outset. This will require a slower, more deliberate pace for any investigation, and a longer period where fewer headlines are generated.

And the data privacy aspects of that business model, while useful for larger policy discussions, may be ill fitting within the narrower legal contours of an antitrust law case. They may be an unnecessary distraction from what ultimately will need to be proven—that there is real, current, and ongoing harm to consumers and advertisers caused by Google's market dominance.

The German case was heralded widely when the Facebook investigation was launched, encouraging the Bundeskartellamt to employ a kitchen-sink approach that included any possible antitrust theory rather than focusing on likely persuasive evidence that could survive a judicial appeal.

If its U.S. state and federal counterparts are to derive any quick lesson from across the Atlantic, it should be that antitrust law, while broadly written, requires a greater level of precision that reflects the technology and business realities of Google and its online competitors, now and in the years to come.

Stuart N. Brotman

Consumer Privacy Protection
May Justify a Big Tech Antitrust Exemption

The global tsunami of Big Tech company antitrust investigations has finally hit. The Department of Justice, the Federal Trade Commission, and virtually all the states have initiated formal inquiries against Amazon, Facebook, and/or Google. Jurisdictional lines also are blurring, making these investigations either more efficient through information sharing or more unwieldy if turf battles break out regarding which agency has primary prosecutorial responsibilities.

And further afield, the European Commission is continuing its antirust focus on the activities of these companies, eager to hear what U.S. antitrust enforcers are discovering. A parallel track of Big Tech scrutiny, particularly in Congress, has been to hold a series of hearings on the effect of competition on data and privacy. The third conclave was held earlier this month by the House antitrust subcommittee, and more Big Tech company representatives can be expected to take their turns at the witness table in the coming weeks and months.

The plethora of antitrust investigations are at early information-gathering stages. The issuance of subpoenas and outreach to Big Tech competitors who are eager to describe in detail how they have been disadvantaged in the marketplace by one or more tech Goliaths illustrates that these are serious pursuits. For now, the only certainty is that any antitrust cases that ultimately may be prosecuted—either by government lawyers or in civil class actions—will take years to be completed. The development of effective remedies is especially complex, even if the end result is either a consent decree or a settlement.

Meanwhile, Big Tech will continue to face serious scrutiny regarding consumer data collection, sharing, and privacy practices. At a practical level, the antitrust investigations are likely to be in the spotlight as vast government and company resources are devoted to them. This makes sense, since the potential antitrust penalties range from multibillion dollar fines to the more severe mandates of partial or complete corporate divestiture. Consequently, companies as well as Congress may move Big Tech data privacy issues to the back burner. Continuous hearings will keep the flame burning in this area, but they may not produce the type of distinct (and headline-grabbing) outcomes that are possible when the Sherman Act and comparable state laws are employed.

This dynamic is not beneficial to millions of American consumers who may view digital privacy as a higher priority than government oversight of Big Tech competition. That's because Big Tech companies, regardless of their size or dominance in the marketplace, are unlikely to adopt privacy practices that others can or will follow. The antitrust laws are actually working against consumer interests by not allowing the largest Big Tech companies to share perspectives on privacy protection measures that they are developing or that already have been put in place.

Counterintuitively, for privacy it would be better public policy for Big Tech companies to be permitted to assemble their own big tent where they can begin discussing collectively their data collection, sharing, and privacy protection regimes. Here, unlike in the antitrust realm, Congress has a central role to play.

It is possible to separate the antirust and privacy concerns in a manner that does not impede the competition investigations. This would take the form of a narrow, time-specific (eighteen- to twenty-four-month) antitrust exemption for the specific purpose of having these companies develop workable consumer data privacy protocols that could be implemented voluntarily on an across-the-board basis throughout the digital ecosystem, rather than in piecemeal fashion.

Big Tech companies may already have antitrust immunity, based on prior judicial rulings, from working together to influence any consumer data privacy policy that may be created in the near future. And Congress has already enacted a series of expansive laws exempting big sports (Major League Baseball and the National Football League), big newspapers (the Newspaper Preservation Act), and big insurers (the McCann-Ferguson Act) from antitrust liability. This means that any potential political blowback for enacting a Big Tech antitrust exemption would be cushioned by ample legal precedent.

My proposal is more modest, with a short-enough sunset period to see if results would be forthcoming. Such an antitrust exemption would be beneficial to Big Tech, too, if it were able to show how joint action provided a workable privacy self-regulatory model, thus making legislation less necessary. On a public perception level, Big Tech would also be able to score some consumer brownie points by developing a suite of privacy solutions that could take hold sooner rather than later.

Congress has the legislative authority to enact a limited antitrust exemption for Big Tech on privacy, but it will need to obtain the support of the Department of Justice (DOJ) to do so. Such a two-step process is welcomed, since the DOJ will be vigilant in ensuring that any exemption not impede the scores of antitrust investigations already underway. In effect, this exemption would enable the tsunami to continue at full force while simultaneously creating some possibility of better consumer data privacy protection.

Admittedly, the legislative details of my proposed antitrust exemption will need to be developed with greater specificity, along with sensitivity to the joint action boundaries that such an exemption would establish.

Although consumer privacy protection would be the ultimate goal, the exemption would not guarantee that Big Tech

companies would work together to use their combined
economies of scale and scope for the public good. But moving in
this direction would provide an effective route forward in at
least one major area of political and social concern about Big
Tech's ever-expanding reach into the daily activities of our lives.

Consumer Privacy Protection
Deserves 5G Policy Attention

Given the serious trade and national security aspects of the development of 5G mobile services, the specter of dominance in network equipment provisioning by Chinese companies, notably Huawei Technologies Co. Ltd. has brought 5G into the national policy spotlight.

Currently, the U.S. is developing a comprehensive 5G strategy under the auspices of the National Economic Council and the National Security Council. In recent testimony before the Senate Homeland Security and Governmental Affairs Committee, Christopher Krebs, director of the U.S. Department of Homeland Security's Cybersecurity and Infrastructure Security Agency, noted "with confidence that the United States is collaborating effectively across agencies and with our industry partners."

Others in the hearing, including Senators Gary Peters (D-MI) and Mitt Romney (R-UT), disagreed by expressing concern that there is no coordinated plan to secure U.S. 5G networks. And Federal Communications Commissioner Jessica Rosenworcel noted the Defense Innovation Board's assessment that "the country that owns 5G will own innovations and set the standards for the rest of the world."

The looming possibility that China, not the U.S., will emerge as the dominant 5G leader worldwide is unprecedented. But the current debate over U.S. readiness largely is reactive, based on a notion that our nation may be playing a losing 5G hand with China.

If there is in fact a comprehensive national policy in the process of being formulated, it needs to include a more holistic view that encompasses both the construction of 5G networks (which also must address vital unresolved spectrum allocation issues) and the consequences of a massive increase in digital information that will flow through them once they are fully operational.

Put simply, the demand side of the 5G equation needs to be taken into account. The development of 5G networks depends upon consumer willingness to pay for 5G service offerings. Here, the U.S. can assume a clear leadership position by focusing on enhanced privacy protection measures that will be offered on these networks.

Since only a handful of telecommunications carriers will have the financial capability to invest in 5G networks, the U.S. is in a unique position as a competitive economy. If consumer privacy protection is articulated in a national 5G strategy, it would send a strong signal that telecom companies can gain a competitive advantage by having them develop more attractive consumer privacy practices as points of marketplace differentiation.

For example, what if an innovative company offered a privacy notice and consent in audio and video formats, including multiple languages, which could be more easily understood by consumers? This could be an attractive feature to those who otherwise would be confronted by pages of dense text that would not be read, and thus not provide adequate transparency.

Or what if a competitor decides to offer an insurance policy that covers major privacy lapses, akin to how trip insurance now is offered routinely when an airline ticket is purchased? These enhancements need not be government mandates, but they certainly would serve the national interest along with business needs. The U.S. can tip the balance back in its favor by focusing on a core national asset—a culture of innovation. In turn, this can lead to our nation setting 5G consumer privacy standards for China and the rest of the world. And by innovating in consumer privacy protection, the robust cybersecurity protection that 5G networks require would also be advanced.

On the equipment side, a more defined U.S. regulatory role by the FCC could help reinforce consumer privacy protection that is offered for 5G services in the competitive marketplace. This might take the form of requiring that all 5G carriers certify to the FCC that the 5G networking equipment they are purchasing is embedded with a set of technical capabilities that will allow the carriers to offer enhanced consumer privacy protection on their 5G networks.

As a practical matter, this would force China and other countries supplying this equipment to conform to a U.S. standard. In turn, this would address the ongoing U.S. national security concerns regarding foreign hardware provisioning and also help the U.S. create a de facto worldwide standard for 5G consumer privacy protection.

Here's the bottom line: regardless of how well the U.S. is developing a national 5G strategy now, it is destined to be incomplete until it articulates consumer privacy (as distinct from cybersecurity) protection as an important variable to consider in the 5G equation.

The 5G privacy opportunity:
Don't just develop wireless data Innovation Zones; focus on protecting personal data, too

Recently, the Federal Communications Commission announced that it would be granting experimental licenses for companies in New York City and Salt Lake City to test new advanced technologies and networks in specific geographic areas.

This initiative, dubbed Innovation Zones, will be especially useful in testing various technologies in real-world settings that will support 5G wireless networks. These networks will offer a range of advanced wireless services nationwide, with initial rollout in urban centers where spatial and population density makes technical and economic sense.

The National Science Foundation's Platform for Advanced Wireless Research formally proposed these particular Innovation Zones, to "enable experimental exploration of robust new wireless devices, communication techniques, networks, systems, and services that will revolutionize the nation's wireless ecosystem, thereby enhancing broadband connectivity, leveraging the emerging Internet of Things, and sustaining U.S. leadership and economic competitiveness for decades to come."

Here's a way that the FCC can use these Innovation Zones for multiple purposes. Since 5G networks will increase consumer demand for new wireless services, they also may create a communications environment where the protection of consumer data becomes more difficult in practice. That's because a range of blossoming wireless services—both free and paid—will combine communications capability with other features, such as location tracking and facial recognition. These are not unique to 5G technology, but its availability will spur big companies and entrepreneurs alike to develop compelling new applications that can take advantage of this more robust wireless platform.

The current Innovation Zone regime will allow qualifying firms to construct testing for multiple non-related experiments under a single five-year authorization within a defined geographic area. The initial two Innovation Zones will allow licensees to undertake their activities in a dense area between Columbia University and Harlem in New York City, encompassing both the University of Utah campus and downtown Salt Lake City, including the corridor connecting the two.

Why not make them data privacy Innovation Zones as well? The FCC, as a condition of granting these experimental licenses, has the legal authority to require that any new wireless services to be tested also experiment with different forms of consumer privacy protection.

Opt ins rather than opt outs for additional features would be useful to evaluate, as would notice and consent terms that use video instead of text to let people know how their data are being collected, stored, and shared. Variations in privacy protection based on whether the service was free or paid (and if paid, with different pricing levels) also may be useful to assess.

Under my proposal, each experimental licensee would be required to indicate the parameters of its privacy protection testing, both to the FCC and to consumers who agree to participate in it.

Just as these licensees will need to report their technical findings, the FCC could require that anonymous aggregated data regarding data privacy experimental options be made available to the agency. This would be useful information to have as the need for new data privacy regulation or legislation is evaluated. The FCC could also share this information with the Federal Trade Commission, the agency that currently has broad federal privacy enforcement authority, along providing it to states that oversee consumer data protection more locally.

Encouraging data privacy experimentation as well as new communication technology testing would make New York City and Salt Lake City, along with other cities that follow, Innovation Zones in a broader and more beneficial way.

Stuart N. Brotman

How Congress Can Take Action
on Strengthening Consumer Privacy

A simple bill to create a National Commission on Consumer Privacy could explore this area with breadth and depth, while building necessary bipartisan consensus for any legislation that may develop down the road.

Commissions such as this must be established formally by Congress, and they have served our country well in providing independent advice and making recommendations for changes in public policy based on expert research, data analysis, and information gained through onsite visits. With consumer privacy top of mind among lawmakers, regulators, businesses, and consumer protection groups, such a commission would be invaluable as an efficient and effective means to explore the issues raised by the Business Roundtable executives, along with others to be added.

As the Congressional Research Service itself has noted, "Throughout American history, Congress has found commissions to be useful tools in the legislative process, and legislators continue to use them today." More than a hundred commissions have been established during the past thirty years, with recent positive examples such as the Creating Options for Veterans Expedited Recovery Commission, the National Commission on Hunger, and the Commission to Eliminate Child Abuse and Neglect Fatalities.

Having a commission before the sausage factory of actual legislation is opened up would provide a highly visible national forum for consumer privacy that marshals more expertise than may be readily available to existing staff in Congress, and enable greater depth than might be practical for lawmakers facing the realities of multitasking on steroids. Historically, commissions have been nonpartisan or bipartisan.

This means that if organized with care, such a commission could make its findings and recommendations more likely to be accepted by the public and embodied in legislation that could be signed into law. Congress would have a sense of ownership from day one, since commission appointees would be selected in part or whole by lawmakers.

There are enough cynics in Washington who would view this proposal as creating just another mini bureaucracy to minimize the chances that anything will really be accomplished. After all, some would argue that if Congress needs to make tough choices regarding consumer privacy legislation, it would be better to do that than establish a commission that it could later disavow in the interest of blame avoidance.

But on balance, and given the impeachment inquiry, a commission on consumer privacy can be designed to be the locomotive for a train already in motion rather than a sidecar that may derail greater oversight. There is no cookie cutter approach for what is needed to create a useful commission, but enabling legislation should be prioritized over moving swiftly to draft, debate, revise, and reconcile actual bills.

The mandate of such a commission, its duties and powers, its membership structure, appointment scheme, and termination date for reporting back to Congress are the obvious places to start. Field hearings by the commission around the country would be especially useful to authorize, since they would enable the commission to hear from diverse stakeholders and generate political capital for the challenging legislative battle that consumer privacy will almost certainly trigger.

A National Commission on Consumer Privacy is a practical measure. This call to action should be well received both in the House and the Senate, and across the political aisle, since Republicans and Democrats alike are keenly interested in exploring workable legislative options.

Stuart N. Brotman

138

How Online Privacy Notices
Can Achieve Better User Consent

Senator Marsha Blackburn (R-TN) introduced the Balancing the Rights of Web Surfers Equally and Responsibly (BROWSER) Act last spring, and it remains dormant in the legislative process for now. Its most salutary provisions deal with online privacy policies, including 1) a requirement, under federal law, that users be provided with "clear and conspicuous notice" of a communications or technology company's consumer data privacy policies; 2) an ability for users to opt in for the collection of sensitive information; and 3) a prohibition of these companies denying service to anyone who refuses to waive privacy rights.

The thorniest of these mandates is the first one, since "clear and conspicuous" is too ambiguous a term. For companies, their main interest is to protect themselves from legal liability, hence the seemingly endless pages of dense text aimed at supporting a claim of a liability waiver if the matter were brought to court. They cannot be faulted for protecting their business interests by having detailed legal language presented before a user clicks an acceptance.

Yet the reality a recently released survey by the respected Pew Research Center indicates is that about 80% of Americans reported that they are asked to agree to an online privacy policy at least monthly, with 25% asked to do so daily. Not surprisingly, fewer than 1 in 5 say they read these privacy policies in full before agreeing to their terms and conditions.

Here are three practical suggestions for improving the BROWSER Act's "clear and conspicuous" privacy notice standard, reflecting marketplace realities and enabling better enforcement by any government agency that is charged with this responsibility.

First, the provision should cover not just websites, but also apps. That's because the main online touchpoint in the U.S. is now a mobile smartphone rather than a desktop or laptop computer with a hardwired broadband connection, according to the research firm Com Score. And eMarketer's 2019 data shows that the average person spends 90% of their mobile time in apps vs. on the mobile web. A law that is aimed at web surfing seems to be as outmoded as dial-up service.

Any online privacy text notice should also contain multiple language capability. U.S. Census data show that at least 15% of our adult population—35 million citizens—speaks a language other than English at home. It's likely that a significant number never have had a chance to read and understand an online privacy notice at all since there is no requirement that versions other than English be made available. Technology provides the ability for such translations to be made with ease.

Finally, in a world where video is increasingly the go-to source for online content, privacy notices should be required to be offered in video format as well as text. According to the research firm Forrester, a one-minute video could contain the equivalent of 3,600 pages of text—way beyond what would be needed to secure meaningful consent.

Video privacy policies are more likely to stick, too. A study by Insivia, for example, found that "viewers retain 95% of a message when they watch it in video." Video notices also could tap into boundless creative elements to enhance attractiveness to users as well as their greater understanding. Some might even go viral.

Cynics might argue that even with these modest modifications, companies still are likely to offer opaque or confusing online privacy notices. But one need not look further than turning on an iPhone to see that it is possible to provide more privacy protection with less verbiage. Apple lets its users know what consumer information the company is not collecting, such as location history, credit and debit card numbers, health records, Siri requests, and Apple News content access. By being upfront in simple language, this approach should serve as a benchmark for how consumers will reward those who are providing "clear and conspicuous" privacy notices.

The needs of communications and technology companies can be met while ensuring greater privacy protection for a better-informed public at large. A revised BROWSER Act can achieve widespread bipartisan acceptance in Congress by being more inclusive and innovative in its approach.

Stuart N. Brotman

Why the New Robocall Law is Important for Future Privacy Legislation

With little congressional movement regarding federal privacy legislation apparent as 2020 begins, those hoping that a new law will be enacted this year are likely to be disappointed.

The external political realities of impeachment, the 2020 elections, and no discernible push for a federal privacy law by the Trump administration suggest a scenario in which this issue will be kicked down the road for a new Congress (and perhaps a new administration) to consider.

But the recent enactment of another federal privacy law—the Telephone Robocall Abuse Criminal Enforcement and Deterrence Act (nicknamed TRACED)—offers some useful lessons about how a piece of privacy legislation can make it to the president's desk.

First, despite the continuing rancor between Republicans and Democrats, TRACED demonstrated that it is possible to achieve broad support for privacy legislation.

The strong leadership shown by Rep. Frank Pallone Jr. (D-NJ) and Sen. John Thune (R-SD) serves as a model for the type of bipartisan, bicameral work that will be needed if future privacy legislation is able to gain necessary momentum. TRACED passed with a 417-3 vote in the House and on a voice vote in the Senate. President Trump then signed it into law.

The second asset that TRACED exhibited is a laser-like approach to a pervasive, real-world privacy problem—

unwanted robocalls—along with targeted solutions to deal with it directly. This narrower scope may be more effective in moving privacy legislation along, rather than starting from a premise that a new law needs to be "comprehensive" in order to be worthy.

Such a broad aspiration sounds good in theory, and may attract initial support and favorable press coverage. But it also may result in a legislative vehicle that is too cumbersome to manage. Inevitably, varying stakeholders will seek to add more to the legislation. That may ultimately doom enactment since too much weight attached to a legislative proposal can make it unpalatable to one or more interest groups.

TRACED avoided this obstacle by developing a good, albeit imperfect, approach that provides greater enforcement powers while also supporting phone company measures already under way to help identify and block robocalls more effectively.

Another important attribute of TRACED that is worthy of emulation is a recognition that enforcement can be a shared responsibility, in this case between the Federal Communications Commission and state attorneys general. Contrast this with the current jurisdictional quagmire that potential privacy legislation is confronting—namely, whether there needs to be federal preemption of state privacy enforcement to achieve a necessary level of uniformity that industry players say is a litmus test for their support.

Finally, TRACED is designed to keep Congress in the loop as the law rolls out, so that it can make adjustments in enforcement requirements and financial penalties based on how effective the new law will be in reducing unwanted robocalls. Call blocking technology is also expected to advance over time, which is another reason TRACED should not be considered as a one-and-done law. Rather, it is an important initial step in legislatively addressing this problem. (The FCC has been doing this for years without useful congressional guidance.) Going forward, privacy legislation should include a requirement of an annual report to

Congress, with public availability. The dynamic nature of the digital marketplace demands no less.

TRACED does not provide an exhaustive view of the building blocks that would be useful to add for future privacy legislation so that it can move from its current stalemated status. The implementation of the California Consumer Privacy Act (CCPA), which became effective on January 1, 2020, may help create more pressure for a federal solution.

But unless Congress looks inward to how it can achieve its own legislative success in this area, the chances that federal privacy legislation will be enacted in 2020 seem small. TRACED offers several elements to an equation that seems essential for any such legislation to be enacted, whether in the 116th Congress or beyond.

Millennials Can Help Grandparents
Achieve Stronger Internet Privacy

It is not Labor Day or Thanksgiving, but National Grandparents Day has been a designated United States holiday for more than forty years. The perfect gift that millennials, those born between 1981 and 1996, can give then to their beloved older relatives is better digital privacy protection.

Millennials, according to a survey by the Pew Research Center, are a digitally savvy generation. More than 90% of millennials own smartphones, and the vast majority at 85% say they use social media. Significantly larger shares of millennials have adopted relatively new platforms such as Instagram and Snapchat than older generations.

In contrast, the survey shows that grandparents, typically members of the silent generation, have not have been as enthusiastic in adopting a range of digital technologies in recent years. Less than a third of silents report owning a smartphone, and even fewer indicate that they have a tablet computer or use social media. Previous surveys by the Pew Research Center have found that the oldest adults face some unique barriers to adopting new technologies, from a lack of confidence in using new technologies to physical challenges manipulating various devices.

Although not quantified, there also is a real fear among silents that they are poorly equipped to navigate their digital devices and online services to provide the necessary privacy protection against online scammers. According to the Federal Bureau of Investigation, "Older Americans are less likely to report a fraud because they do not know who to report it to, are too ashamed at having been scammed, or do not know they have been scammed. Elderly victims may not report crimes, for example, because they are concerned that relatives may think victims no longer have the mental capacity to take care of their own financial affairs."

That brings us to a gift recommendation for all millennials on National Grandparents Day, which is an emailed card with a coupon for a one-hour visit. When it is redeemed, focus on some key aspects of online privacy protection that can offer grandparents an increased level of confidence in connecting to the amazing digital capabilities that the Internet offers.

Start with a conversation about how they are engaging online now and what they would like to do to make them they feel better about privacy concerns. Work with them on developing a series of passwords that will not be easy for someone to discover. Tell them to forget about family names, birthdates, anniversaries, or expressions like "I love you." A few complex passwords, such as their high school mascots combined with their graduation years, should do the trick with their recall, but write passwords down in a journal that will be handy if memory is fuzzy.

Encourage them to only use credit cards for online shopping, which have a high level of transactional security. Using them instead of debit cards is the way to go, since there is a maximum liability of $50 for fraudulent charges and the ability to report them to the card issuer, which has a whole department to investigate and resolve unauthorized charges.

Show them the difference between a genuine trusted website and one that is fraudulent. For example, an email received from www.irs.gov is an official one sent by the Internal Revenue Service, while something from www.irs.us is a scam. Have them email or text you before they open anything that looks suspicious if there is any doubt so you can advise them accordingly.

Customize their security settings for each of their devices, including browser controls that allow websites to track cookies, the tiny files that are transferred to a computer from a visited website.

Better online privacy protection can be passed up from younger to older generations, in a welcome reversal of the traditional pattern of elders handing their wisdom down to the offspring of their offspring. This gift is guaranteed to be greatly appreciated for both its novelty and utility. It can also help to forge more frequent communication afterwards between millennials and grandparents that is meaningful throughout the year.

Stuart N. Brotman

Let's Get America's Internet Nonusers Online Now

In these dark days of COVID-19, we quickly have become an online country. Millions of workers now are away from their offices working remotely via the Internet, while they and those not in the workforce continue to rely intensively on an online umbilical cord—often wireless—for vital news and information about the pandemic. Digital connections also enable us to be in touch seamlessly with family and friends during this crisis, which is essential to our overall well-being.

Numerous analysts have pointed out the persistent digital divide we face—namely, that at least 20 million American households currently lack broadband Internet access. This divide is especially pronounced in rural areas and among those who are not benefitting from an existing federal Lifeline program that subsidizes Internet access at home. This is a real problem that extends to both those who are unserved and underserved online.

But less publicized, although perhaps easier to address now in real time, is the portion of our population that already has residential broadband capability, but somehow believes there is no value in connecting. It may be shocking to realize that 10% of U.S. adults, according to the Pew Research Center, are not using the Internet at all. This figure has been relatively static for over four years. We need to focus immediate attention on how to begin flattening that curve, too.

That's because there continues to be a drop off in those 65 and older who never go online—27% of them in the latest Pew Center survey. This age group also is at the highest medical risk for contracting COVID-19, and would benefit greatly by access to vital health and safety information on a 24/7 basis.

There also are economic implications to refusing to go online, again hurting those who may benefit tremendously from Internet connections. In addition to health and safety information, telework largely requires such connections. Those who are unwilling to undertake getting them, especially when the cost may be subsidized by an employer, are increasing the likelihood that they will be considered more expendable in the workforce. Yet according to the Pew Center data, roughly 3 in 10 adults with less than a high school education do not use the Internet.

Other demographic analyses highlight disparities based on household income and community type; various factors are at play regarding why this problem exists. The important point to focus on now is developing practical ways to reduce the percentage of nationwide Internet nonusers as soon as possible, so that we have a broader population base who can take advantage of the Internet's information and communications capabilities.

Traditional mass media may be the best route to let nonusers know why the national effort to combat the pandemic requires them to go online. Companies can help underwrite public service ads in print and on radio and television to creatively get this message out. Public health officials, government leaders, family members, and neighbors also can be part of a coordinated "get online now" campaign.

Although this will not alleviate concerns about those without broadband availability, such a campaign at least could help persuade millions of Americans that it is both in their self-interest and in the national interest to join an online community that welcomes them now in a time of great collective need.

Acknowledgments

This book is a real-time exploration of thinking about digital privacy policy, reflecting the work undertaken during my extraordinary residency at the Wilson Center. There, I was provided with a nurturing environment for my research and writing and a wonderful base for me to gather and share thoughts from leading thinkers and policymakers in this area, both in the United States and throughout the world.

The Wilson Center, since its inception over fifty years ago, creates connections between scholarship and policy. It offers a forum for actionable ideas—whether they were hatched in government, academia, or the business community. The need for nonpartisan scholarship and policy ideas is urgent, and as noted by its director, president, and CEO, Jane Harman, "The Wilson Center remains totally committed to its mission of creating knowledge in the public service, along with providing a real 'safe political space' that has to be safe for controversial ideas."

The Wilson Center encouraged me to think broadly and deeply, with room to explore my research without limitation. A wealth of resources was made available, including the unparalleled collections at the Library of Congress, and the ability to interact, through meetings and center events, with a wide range of individuals who helped inform and enlarge my perspectives in many ways.

The output of Wilson Center fellows throughout its history is impressive—hundreds of books that are based on their activities while in residence. These volumes are displayed prominently on ever-expanding shelves in the center's library. Most importantly, they reflect the Wilson Center's enduring mission of creating knowledge in the public service.

This book represents the culmination of my Wilson Center fellowship. While each of the pieces can be read on its own, collectively the whole here is greater than the sum of its parts. I am pleased that my contribution will find a place on the center's shelves in its library, which houses the many other books by Wilson Center fellows, and in the Library of Congress.

As a 2019–20 Fellow, based in the center's interdisciplinary Science and Technology Innovation Program, I faced an unprecedented situation when the center moved to remote telework in March 2020 as the intensity of the COVID-19 pandemic became apparent. Ironically, the pandemic brought an even greater sense of urgency to my work there. I completed many new published pieces regarding implications for a world that surely will change over the coming weeks and years in its aftermath. In turn, I present a longer view looking ahead to reflect digital privacy policy in post-pandemic times.

My deep appreciation is extended to the entire Wilson Center family, with special recognition to Director, President, and CEO Jane Harman; Director of the Science and Technology Innovation Program Meg King; Senior Vice President for Scholars and Administration Robert Litwak; Fellowship Specialist Kimberly Conner; and Information Receptionist Lindsay Collins.

Others at the Wilson Center served as sounding boards for me, and valued colleagues in every sense. They include John Milewski, Ryan McKenna, Molly Heinsler, Janet Spikes, Anne Bowser, Steve Lagerfeld, Elinor Harty, John Tyler, and Ruth Greenspan Bell. John Dale, Wenhong Chen, Richard Tomlinson, Camelia Bogdan, Mitchell Reiss, and Jeremy Spaulding also were outstanding in providing valued advice throughout the year. Meghan Lewis provided able research assistance, as well.

I also appreciate the support of those at the University of Tennessee, Knoxville who enabled me to take a research leave for the academic year to serve as a Wilson Center Fellow, in particular Mike Wirth, Dean of the College of Communication and Information, and Catherine Luther, Director of the School of Journalism and Electronic Media.

Nell Minow, Mira Singer, and David Apatoff of Miniver Press, a unique author-centered publisher, have been invaluable in providing editorial and graphic advice with such careful attention to details. This book would not have been possible without them.

A number of pieces benefitted from the fine editorial review of Anjelica Tan, Shawn McCoy, Ray Walker, Kate Patrick, Sherry Kim, Vandana Sinha, Joseph Blake, and Michael Demenchuk.

There are numerous professional colleagues and friends who provided great input and feedback along the way, including some who I have known for many years and others who I was fortunate to encounter while in residence at the Wilson Center. They include Blair Levin, Genie Barton, Jules Polonetsky, Richard Kaplar, Gabriela Oliván, Jon Adame, Dom Caristi, Ken Basin, Alex Heaton, Patrick Burkart, Ari Waldman, Howard Homonoff, Peter Swire, Parry Aftab, Nuala O'Connor, Larry Lichty, Bruce Goodman, Beverly Banks, Bert Fields, Barbara Guggenheim, Randy Tritell, Brian Wesolowski, David Cantor, Eric Burger, Barbara Kelly, Ron Rizzuto, Gracia Carvallo, Rick Schultz, Sandra Baer, Stuart Ingis, Larry Taymor, David Grimaldi, Sanford Ungar, Michael Fricklas, Stan Pierre-Louis, Jonathan Adelstein, Norm Coleman, Denis McDonough, Coleman Bazelon, Michael Nelson, Giulia McHenry, Patricia Phelan, Brett Perlman, Christopher Wolf, Cam Kerry, Kenneth Marcus, Bonnie Eskenazi, Joseph Fishman, Urs Gasser, Howard Liberman, Margaret Whitehead, Elaine Joyce, Barry Umansky, Adam Zuckerman, John Flynn, Martha Minow, Anne Klinefelter, Ken Kaufman, Lucy Dalglish, Samantha Levin, Larry Strickling, Nana Sarian, Ron Cass, Joyce Rechstaffen, Bruce Malashevich, John Hane, Nick Depperschmidt, Howard Homonoff, Mark

Itkin, Larry Chalfin, Jack Moline, Päivi Korpisaari, Andy Cohen, Cornell Christianson, Kitty Ganier, Bob Males, Mark Seidenfeld, Sandra Bresnick, Gary Arlen, Bob Stearns, Deborah Grosvenor, Erwin Chemerinsky, Bob Katz, Kerry Moynihan, Susan Kohler Reed, Mary Minow, Colette Seidel, Jerry Fritz, Deb Gordon, Olaf Groth, Larry Irving, Jim Chiddix, Roslyn Layton, Michele Farquhar, Margaret Hu, Bill Zarakas, Margery Kraus, Dan Scandling, Brent Crane, Rob Frieden, Ron Kovac, Clare Sullivan, Peter Gross, and Miriam Berg.

Newton N. Minow has been a major influence and role model for virtually all of my career, and I am honored that he agreed to contribute so thoughtfully to this book. Sadly, three other brilliant lawyers and friends passed away shortly before this book's completion, and their inspiration lives on. Morton Hamburg, Henry Geller, and Joel Reidenberg left enduring marks and are remembered fondly for their intellect and humanity.

As always, my wife Gloria Z. Greenfield, and children Daniel, Rachel, and Gabriel provided me with familial warmth and comfort, especially welcomed during a year largely spent away from them.

The views expressed throughout are to be attributed solely to me, and all errors or omissions are mine, too. I welcome reactions to any of my ideas here, including additional thoughts to consider as we all continue to navigate through Privacy's Perfect Storm.

Stuart N. Brotman
sbrotman@brotman.com

July 2020

About the Author

Stuart N. Brotman served as a 2019–20 Fellow in the Science and Technology Innovation Program at the Woodrow Wilson International Center for Scholars in Washington, DC, focusing on digital privacy policy issues.

He is one of the leading global experts in this area, and has published widely on digital privacy and cybersecurity topics, including in the *Columbia Journal of International Affairs*, the *Fletcher Forum of Global Affairs*, the *Vanderbilt Journal of Entertainment and Technology Law*, *The Hill*, *Government Executive*, *Inside Sources*, *The Urbanist*, *Bloomberg Law*, the *New York Daily News*, and the *San Francisco Chronicle*. His media appearances in this area have included the Canadian Broadcast Corporation, National Public Radio, Voice of America, and Yahoo News. He serves on the Advisory Board of the Future of Privacy Forum.

Brotman is an American government policymaker, tenured university professor, management consultant, lawyer, author, editorial adviser, and nonprofit organization executive. He has served in four presidential administrations on a bipartisan basis and has taught students from forty-two countries in six separate disciplines—communications, journalism, business, law, international relations, and public policy. He also has advised private and public sector clients in more than thirty countries on five continents.

He is the inaugural Howard Distinguished Endowed Professor of Media Management and Law and Beaman Professor of Journalism and Electronic Media at the University of Tennessee, Knoxville. He also served as the Fulbright-Nokia Distinguished Chair in Information and Communications Technologies at the University of Helsinki.

Brotman served on the founding leadership team as Special Assistant to the President's principal communications policy adviser and Chief of Staff at the National Telecommunications and Information Administration (NTIA) in Washington, DC. In this capacity, he worked closely with the White House, Congress, the FCC, FTC, the U.S. Department of Justice, other executive branch departments, independent agencies, and the research and academic communities in developing durable models for telecommunications and information convergence.

He was the first Harvard Law School faculty member to teach telecommunications law, and to serve there as a Visiting Professor of Entertainment and Media Law. He also served as a faculty member in Harvard Law School's Institute for Global Law and Policy and in the Harvard Business School Executive Education Program. He held the first concurrent appointment in digital media at Harvard and MIT, respectively at the Berkman Klein Center for Internet & Society and the Program on Comparative Media Studies, and created the first study group on communications policymaking at the Harvard Kennedy School Institute of Politics.

Brotman serves on APCO Worldwide's International Advisory Council. He is a Distinguished Fellow at The Media Institute and an Eisenhower Fellow. He also served as a Research Fellow at The Aspen Institute; a Nonresident Senior Fellow in the Government Studies Program Center for Technology Innovation at The Brookings Institution; an Information Technology Fellow at the Center for Strategic and International Studies; and a Senior Fellow at Northwestern University's Annenberg Washington Program in Communications Policy Studies.

He is the author of *Communications Law and Practice,* the leading comprehensive treatise covering telecommunications and electronic media.

www.ingramcontent.com/pod-product-compliance
Lightning Source LLC
Chambersburg PA
CBHW060456280326
41933CB00014B/2765